THE PSYCHOLOGY OF FINANCE

Understand the Psychological Influences of Financial Decision-making

Dr. Maxwell Shimba

Shimba Publishing, LLC
Printed in the United States of America

First Printing Edition 2024

TABLE OF CONTENTS

INTRODUCTION

The interplay between psychology and finance is a fascinating field that delves into how human behavior affects financial decisions and markets. This book, "The Psychology of Finance," aims to uncover the psychological principles that drive our financial choices, exploring both individual and collective behaviors. Understanding these principles can lead to more informed financial decisions, improved investment strategies, and better management of personal and corporate finances.

The Intersection of Psychology and Finance

At first glance, psychology and finance may appear to be two disparate fields. Psychology focuses on understanding human behavior and mental processes, while finance is concerned with the management of money, investments, and financial systems. However, these two disciplines are intimately connected. Financial decisions are ultimately made by individuals whose behaviors and thought processes are influenced by psychological factors.

In the world of finance, decisions are often made under conditions of uncertainty and risk. Investors, traders, and financial managers are continually faced with choices that involve predicting future outcomes, assessing risks, and evaluating rewards. Psychological factors such as emotions, cognitive biases, and social influences play a critical role in how these decisions are made.

Behavioral Economics: Bridging the Gap

The field of behavioral economics has emerged as a bridge between psychology and finance. Behavioral economics incorporates insights from psychology to explain why individuals often make irrational financial decisions. Traditional economic theories assume that people are rational actors who always make decisions that maximize their utility. However, behavioral economics recognizes that human behavior is often influenced by irrational and emotional factors.

One of the pioneers of behavioral economics, Daniel Kahneman, along with his colleague Amos Tversky, developed the concept of prospect theory. Prospect theory suggests that people value gains and losses differently, leading to decision-making that deviates from rationality. This theory helps explain why individuals might avoid risks in some situations but embrace them in others, depending on how potential outcomes are framed.

The Influence of Cognitive Biases

Cognitive biases are systematic patterns of deviation from rationality in judgment. These biases affect how we process information, make decisions, and interact with the world around us. In the realm of finance, cognitive biases can lead to suboptimal investment choices, market anomalies, and financial mismanagement.

For example, the overconfidence bias leads investors to overestimate their knowledge and abilities, often resulting in excessive risk-taking and poor investment performance. The anchoring bias causes individuals to rely too heavily on the first piece of information they encounter, even when it is irrelevant to the decision at hand. Understanding these biases and their impact on financial behavior is crucial for making more rational and informed decisions.

The Role of Emotions in Financial Decision-Making

Emotions play a significant role in financial decision-making. Fear, greed, excitement, and regret are just a few of the emotions that can influence how we make financial choices. During periods of market volatility, emotions can drive irrational behaviors such as panic selling or euphoric buying, leading to market bubbles and crashes.

Emotional intelligence, the ability to recognize and manage one's emotions, is a valuable skill in finance. Individuals with high emotional intelligence are better equipped to make rational decisions, even in the face of emotional challenges. Developing emotional intelligence can help investors and financial professionals navigate the emotional ups and downs of the financial markets.

Social Influences and Herd Behavior

Human behavior is profoundly influenced by social factors. Social norms, peer pressure, and the behavior of others can significantly impact our financial decisions. In financial markets, herd behavior occurs when individuals mimic the actions of a larger group, often leading to market trends that are not based on fundamental values.

Herd behavior can contribute to the formation of market bubbles, where asset prices are driven to unsustainable levels by collective enthusiasm. Conversely, it can also lead to market crashes when panic spreads among investors. Understanding the dynamics of social influences and herd behavior is essential for recognizing and mitigating the risks associated with these phenomena.

Financial Personality and Individual Differences

Each individual has a unique financial personality that shapes their approach to money management, risk tolerance, and investment strategies. Factors such as upbringing, life experiences, and inherent personality traits contribute to one's financial behavior. Identifying and understanding one's financial personality can lead to more tailored and effective financial strategies.

For instance, some individuals may have a high risk tolerance and be comfortable with aggressive investment strategies, while others may prefer more conservative approaches. Recognizing these differences can help individuals align their financial decisions with their personal goals and risk preferences.

The Impact of Life Events

Major life events, such as marriage, divorce, retirement, and economic crises, can have a profound impact on financial behavior. These events often bring about significant changes in financial circumstances, necessitating adjustments in financial planning and decision-making. The psychological stress associated with life transitions can also influence financial choices.

For example, the loss of a job can lead to heightened financial anxiety and risk-averse behavior, while receiving a windfall inheritance might prompt more risk-seeking behavior. Understanding the psychological impact of life events can help individuals and financial advisors develop strategies to navigate these transitions effectively.

The Importance of Financial Education

Financial literacy is essential for making informed financial decisions and achieving psychological well-being. A lack of financial knowledge can lead to poor financial choices, increased stress, and diminished financial security. Financial education empowers individuals to understand complex financial concepts, make informed decisions, and take control of their financial futures.

Promoting financial literacy involves providing individuals with the tools and resources they need to understand financial products, manage debt, save for the future, and invest wisely. By enhancing financial education, we can improve financial well-being and reduce the prevalence of financial mismanagement.

Conclusion

The field of financial psychology provides valuable insights into the human aspects of financial decision-making. By understanding the psychological principles that drive our financial behaviors, we can make more informed choices, avoid common pitfalls, and achieve greater financial stability and success. This book aims to equip readers with the knowledge and tools needed to navigate the complex world of finance with confidence and clarity. Through the exploration of behavioral economics, cognitive biases, emotional influences, social factors, and individual differences, we will uncover the intricate interplay between psychology and finance, paving the way for more rational and effective financial decision-making.

DR. MAXWELL SHIMBA

CHAPTER 1

WHAT IS THE PSYCHOLOGY OF FINANCE?

The term "Psychology of Finance" refers to the study of how psychological factors influence financial behavior and decision-making. It encompasses a wide range of topics, including cognitive biases, emotions, social influences, and individual differences. By examining the intersection of psychology and finance, we can gain a deeper understanding of why people make certain financial choices and how these choices impact markets and economic systems.

Understanding Behavioral Economics

Behavioral economics is a key component of the psychology of finance. It challenges the traditional economic assumption that individuals are always rational actors who seek to maximize their utility. Instead, behavioral economics recognizes that human behavior is often influenced by irrational and emotional factors.

Daniel Kahneman and Amos Tversky, two pioneers in this field, developed the concept of prospect theory, which explains how people make decisions involving risk and uncertainty. According to prospect theory, individuals value gains and losses differently, leading to decision-making that deviates from rationality. For example, people tend to be risk-averse when it comes to gains but risk-seeking when trying to avoid losses.

Cognitive Biases and Financial Decision-Making

Cognitive biases are systematic patterns of deviation from rationality in judgment. These biases affect how we process information and make decisions. In finance, cognitive biases can lead to suboptimal investment choices and market anomalies. Here are some common cognitive biases that impact financial behavior:

- Overconfidence Bias: This bias leads individuals to overestimate their knowledge and abilities. Overconfident investors may take on excessive risk, believing they can predict market movements accurately.

- Anchoring Bias: Anchoring occurs when individuals rely too heavily on the first piece of information they encounter. In finance, this might mean sticking to an initial stock price or forecast, even when new information suggests otherwise.

- Confirmation Bias: People tend to seek out information that confirms their existing beliefs and ignore information that contradicts them. This bias can lead to poor investment decisions as investors cling to their preconceived notions.

- Loss Aversion: Individuals experience losses more intensely than gains of the same magnitude. This can lead to risk-averse behavior, such as holding onto losing investments for too long to avoid realizing a loss.

The Role of Emotions in Finance

Emotions play a crucial role in financial decision-making. Fear, greed, excitement, and regret can significantly influence how individuals make financial choices. During periods of market volatility, emotions can drive irrational behaviors such as panic selling or euphoric buying, leading to market bubbles and crashes.

Emotional intelligence, the ability to recognize and manage one's emotions, is a valuable skill in finance. Individuals with high emotional intelligence are better equipped to make rational decisions, even in the face of emotional challenges. Developing emotional intelligence can help investors and financial professionals navigate the emotional ups and downs of the financial markets.

Social Influences and Herd Behavior

Human behavior is profoundly influenced by social factors. Social norms, peer pressure, and the behavior of others can significantly impact our financial decisions. In financial markets, herd behavior occurs when individuals mimic the actions of a larger group, often leading to market trends that are not based on fundamental values.

Herd behavior can contribute to the formation of market bubbles, where asset prices are driven to unsustainable levels by collective enthusiasm. Conversely, it can also lead to market crashes when panic spreads among investors. Understanding the dynamics of social influences and herd behavior is essential for recognizing and mitigating the risks associated with these phenomena.

Financial Personality and Individual Differences

Each individual has a unique financial personality that shapes their approach to money management, risk tolerance, and investment strategies. Factors such as upbringing, life experiences, and inherent personality traits contribute to one's financial behavior. Identifying and understanding one's financial personality can lead to more tailored and effective financial strategies.

For instance, some individuals may have a high-risk tolerance and be comfortable with aggressive investment strategies, while others may prefer more conservative approaches. Recognizing these differences can help individuals align their financial decisions with their personal goals and risk preferences.

The Impact of Life Events on Financial Behavior

Major life events, such as marriage, divorce, retirement, and economic crises, can have a profound impact on financial behavior. These events often bring about significant changes in financial circumstances, necessitating adjustments in financial planning and decision-making. The psychological stress associated with life transitions can also influence financial choices.

For example, the loss of a job can lead to heightened financial anxiety and risk-averse behavior, while receiving a windfall inheritance might prompt more risk-seeking behavior. Understanding the psychological impact of life events can help individuals and financial advisors develop strategies to navigate these transitions effectively.

The Importance of Financial Education

Financial literacy is essential for making informed financial decisions and achieving psychological well-being. A lack of financial knowledge can lead to poor financial choices, increased stress, and diminished financial security. Financial education empowers individuals to understand complex financial concepts, make informed decisions, and take control of their financial futures.

Promoting financial literacy involves providing individuals with the tools and resources they need to understand financial products, manage debt, save for the future, and invest wisely. By enhancing financial education, we can improve financial well-being and reduce the prevalence of financial mismanagement.

Conclusion

The psychology of finance provides valuable insights into the human aspects of financial decision-making. By understanding the psychological principles that drive our financial behaviors, we can make more informed choices, avoid common pitfalls, and achieve greater financial stability and success. This chapter has introduced the key concepts of behavioral economics, cognitive biases, emotional influences, social factors, and individual differences that shape our financial decisions. As we delve deeper into these topics in the following chapters, we will uncover the intricate interplay between psychology and finance, paving the way for more rational and effective financial decision-making.

CHAPTER 02

COGNITIVE BIASES IN THE PSYCHOLOGY OF FINANCE

Cognitive biases are systematic patterns of deviation from rationality in judgment. These biases affect how we process information, make decisions, and interact with the world around us. In the realm of finance, cognitive biases can lead to suboptimal investment choices, market anomalies, and financial mismanagement. Understanding these biases and their impact on financial behavior is crucial for making more rational and informed decisions.

Understanding Cognitive Biases

Cognitive biases stem from the brain's attempt to simplify information processing. While these mental shortcuts, or heuristics, can be useful in everyday decision-making, they can lead to significant errors when applied to complex financial decisions. Cognitive biases can be grouped into several categories based on how they affect financial behavior.

Common Cognitive Biases in Finance

Overconfidence Bias

Overconfidence bias leads individuals to overestimate their knowledge, abilities, and the accuracy of their predictions. In finance, overconfident investors may take on excessive risk, believing they can consistently outperform the market. This bias often results in poor investment performance, as overconfident individuals are more likely to engage in speculative trading and make hasty decisions without adequate research.

Example: An investor may believe they have a unique insight into a particular stock and invest heavily in it, only to face significant losses when the stock does not perform as expected.

Anchoring Bias

Anchoring bias occurs when individuals rely too heavily on the first piece of information they encounter, even if it is irrelevant or misleading. In financial decision-making, this can lead to skewed judgments and suboptimal choices. For instance, an investor might anchor to a stock's initial price and ignore subsequent information that suggests a change in its value.

Example: If a stock was initially valued at $100 but has since dropped to $50 due to poor performance, an investor anchored to the original price might hold onto the stock, expecting it to rebound to $100, despite evidence suggesting otherwise.

Confirmation Bias

Confirmation bias is the tendency to seek out and favor information that confirms one's preexisting beliefs while ignoring or dismissing contradictory evidence. This bias can lead to a skewed perception of reality and reinforce poor financial decisions. Investors with confirmation bias may selectively gather data that supports their investment choices, leading to overconfidence and increased risk.

Example: An investor who believes in the potential of a particular technology might only read positive news articles about companies in that sector, ignoring warnings or negative reports.

Loss Aversion

Loss aversion refers to the tendency to experience losses more intensely than gains of the same magnitude. This bias can lead to risk-averse behavior, such as holding onto losing investments for too long to avoid realizing a loss. It can also result in missed opportunities for potential gains, as individuals become overly cautious.

Example: An investor might refuse to sell a declining stock because selling would mean acknowledging a loss, even though holding onto the stock could lead to further losses.

Herd Behavior

Herd behavior occurs when individuals mimic the actions of a larger group, often leading to market trends that are not based on fundamental values. This bias can drive asset prices to unsustainable levels (bubbles) or cause sharp declines (crashes) as investors follow the crowd rather than make independent, rational decisions.

Example: During a market rally, investors might buy into stocks simply because everyone else is, driving prices up without regard to the underlying value of the companies.

The Impact of Cognitive Biases on Financial Markets

Cognitive biases not only affect individual investors but also have broader implications for financial markets. When many investors exhibit similar biases, their collective behavior can lead to market anomalies such as bubbles and crashes. Understanding these biases can help explain why markets sometimes behave irrationally and why certain investment strategies may succeed or fail.

Market Bubbles

Market bubbles occur when asset prices are driven to unsustainable levels by exuberant investor behavior. Cognitive biases such as overconfidence, confirmation bias, and herd behavior contribute to the formation of bubbles. Investors become overly optimistic, ignoring warning signs and driving prices higher through speculative buying.

Example: The dot-com bubble of the late 1990s was fueled by overconfidence in the potential of internet companies, leading to excessive investment in tech stocks despite a lack of fundamental value.

Market Crashes

Market crashes happen when the inflated prices of assets suddenly collapse, often triggered by a loss of investor confidence. Cognitive biases like loss aversion and herd behavior can exacerbate market declines as investors rush to sell off assets, creating a downward spiral.

Example: The 2008 financial crisis was marked by a sudden loss of confidence in mortgage-backed securities, leading to a massive sell-off and a sharp decline in market values.

Strategies for Mitigating Cognitive Biases

While it is impossible to completely eliminate cognitive biases, awareness and strategic interventions can help mitigate their impact on financial decision-making. Here are some strategies to reduce the influence of cognitive biases:

Diversification

Diversifying investments can help reduce the impact of individual biases on overall portfolio performance. By spreading investments across different asset classes and sectors, investors can protect themselves from the effects of overconfidence and confirmation bias.

Systematic Decision-Making

Adopting a systematic approach to financial decision-making can help counteract the influence of cognitive biases. This involves setting clear investment criteria, following a disciplined process, and relying on data-driven analysis rather than emotional or instinctual reactions.

Seeking Diverse Perspectives

Consulting with financial advisors or engaging in discussions with peers can provide alternative viewpoints and help counter confirmation bias. Diverse perspectives can challenge existing beliefs and lead to more balanced and informed decisions.

Continuous Education

Continuous learning about cognitive biases and their impact on financial behavior can increase awareness and improve decision-making. Staying informed about behavioral finance research and seeking educational resources can help individuals recognize and manage their biases.

Conclusion

Cognitive biases are inherent in human decision-making processes and have a profound impact on financial behavior. By understanding these biases and their effects, investors can develop strategies to mitigate their influence and make more rational and informed financial decisions. Awareness of cognitive biases, coupled with disciplined and systematic approaches to investing, can lead to improved financial outcomes and greater market stability. This chapter has explored the key cognitive biases that affect financial decision-making, providing a foundation for a deeper exploration of psychological principles in finance.

CHAPTER 03

COGNITIVE BIASES IN THE PSYCHOLOGY OF MONEY

Cognitive biases are systematic patterns of deviation from norm or rationality in judgment that affect how people perceive and make money decisions. These biases can lead to irrational financial behavior, such as overspending, inadequate saving, and poor investment choices. Understanding cognitive biases in the context of the psychology of money is essential for making more rational and informed financial decisions. This chapter explores common cognitive biases, their impact on financial behavior, and strategies for recognizing and mitigating their effects.

Common Cognitive Biases in the Psychology of Money

1. Overconfidence Bias

Overconfidence bias leads individuals to overestimate their financial knowledge and abilities. This bias can result in taking on excessive risks and making uninformed financial decisions.

Impact on Financial Behavior:

- Overconfident individuals may engage in speculative investments without adequate research.

- They may underestimate the likelihood of financial setbacks, leading to insufficient savings.

Example: An investor might believe they can consistently outperform the market and make risky trades without considering potential losses.

Mitigation Strategies:

- Seek Diverse Opinions: Consult with financial advisors or trusted individuals to gain different perspectives.

- Stay Humble: Recognize the limits of your financial knowledge and be open to learning.

- Regularly Review Performance: Compare your actual financial outcomes with your expectations to gauge the accuracy of your predictions.

2. Anchoring Bias

Anchoring bias occurs when individuals rely too heavily on the first piece of information they encounter, which can skew their financial decisions.

Impact on Financial Behavior:

- People might base their spending and saving decisions on initial prices or values, ignoring subsequent information.

- They may hold onto outdated financial beliefs or strategies.

Example: A person might stick to an old budget or investment strategy, even when new financial information suggests a change is needed.

Mitigation Strategies:

- Update Information Regularly: Continuously seek out new financial information and adjust your decisions accordingly.

- Consider Multiple Data Points: Avoid making decisions based on a single piece of information by evaluating various factors.

- Reassess Regularly: Periodically review your financial strategies and be willing to make changes.

3. Confirmation Bias

Confirmation bias is the tendency to seek out information that confirms existing beliefs while ignoring or dismissing contradictory evidence.

Impact on Financial Behavior:

- Investors might only seek out positive news about their investments, ignoring warning signs.

- Individuals may stick to ineffective financial habits because they only acknowledge supporting evidence.

Example: A person who believes in the long-term growth of a particular stock might ignore negative reports and continue investing, despite clear signs of decline.

Mitigation Strategies:

- Challenge Your Beliefs: Actively seek out information that contradicts your current financial beliefs and consider it objectively.

- Diversify Information Sources: Use multiple, credible sources to gather a balanced view.

- Engage in Critical Thinking: Evaluate all information critically, regardless of whether it supports or contradicts your beliefs.

4. Loss Aversion

Loss aversion refers to the tendency to experience losses more intensely than gains of the same magnitude, leading to risk-averse behavior.

Impact on Financial Behavior:

- People may avoid selling and losing investments to avoid realizing a loss.

- They might pass up profitable opportunities due to fear of potential losses.

Example: An investor might hold onto a stock that has lost value, hoping it will rebound, rather than accepting the loss and reallocating the funds.

Mitigation Strategies:

- Focus on Long-Term Goals: Keep your long-term financial objectives in mind to avoid making decisions based on short-term losses.

- Reframe Your Perspective: View potential losses as part of the investment process and focus on overall portfolio performance.

- Set Predefined Rules: Establish clear rules for when to sell investments, such as stop-loss orders, to reduce emotional decision-making.

5. Mental Accounting

Mental accounting is the tendency to categorize money into different accounts based on subjective criteria, leading to irrational financial behavior.

Impact on Financial Behavior:

- People may treat money differently depending on its source or intended use, leading to suboptimal financial decisions.

- They might overspend "found money" like bonuses or gifts while being frugal with their regular income.

Example: An individual might splurge with a tax refund while being overly cautious with their paycheck.

Mitigation Strategies:

- Treat All Money Equally: View all financial resources as part of a single portfolio, regardless of their source.

- Create a Comprehensive Budget: Develop a budget that integrates all income and expenses to ensure consistent financial management.

- Prioritize Goals: Allocate money based on financial priorities rather than arbitrary categories.

6. The Endowment Effect

The endowment effect is the tendency to overvalue assets simply because they are owned, leading to irrational attachment and reluctance to sell.

Impact on Financial Behavior:

- Investors may hold onto underperforming assets due to emotional attachment.

- They might refuse to sell assets, even when it would be financially beneficial to do so.

Example: A person might keep a car they rarely use because of sentimental value, even though selling it would free up funds for better uses.

Mitigation Strategies:

- Objective Evaluation: Regularly assess the value and performance of your assets objectively.

- Consider Opportunity Cost: Evaluate the potential benefits of selling assets versus keeping them.

- Seek External Opinions: Consult with others to gain an unbiased perspective on your assets.

Recognizing and Overcoming Cognitive Biases

Recognizing cognitive biases is the first step toward overcoming them. By being aware of these biases, individuals can take proactive steps to mitigate their effects and make more rational financial decisions.

Strategies for Recognizing Cognitive Biases

1. Self-Reflection: Regularly reflect on your financial decisions and identify patterns that may indicate cognitive biases.

- Example: Keep a financial journal to track your decisions and the reasoning behind them. Review it periodically to identify any biases.

2. Seek Feedback: Engage with financial advisors, peers, or mentors to get feedback on your financial decisions.

- Example: Discuss your investment strategies with a financial advisor to identify any potential biases and get objective advice.

3. Continuous Education: Stay informed about cognitive biases and their impact on financial behavior through books, articles, and courses.

- Example: Read books on behavioral finance to deepen your understanding of cognitive biases and how to overcome them.

Strategies for Overcoming Cognitive Biases

1. Develop a Structured Decision-Making Process: Follow a systematic approach to financial decision-making that includes gathering information, evaluating options, and considering potential outcomes.

- Example: Use a decision matrix to weigh the pros and cons of different investment options before making a choice.

2. Set Clear Financial Goals: Establish specific, measurable, achievable, relevant, and time-bound (SMART) financial goals to guide your decisions.

- Example: Set a goal to save a certain amount for retirement within a specified timeframe and create a plan to achieve it.

3. Diversify Your Portfolio: Diversify your investments to spread risk and reduce the impact of cognitive biases on your overall financial performance.

- Example: Invest in a mix of asset classes, such as stocks, bonds, and real estate, to minimize risk and maximize returns.

4. Use Technology: Leverage financial tools and technology to assist with decision-making and reduce the influence of cognitive biases.

- Example: Use budgeting apps to track expenses and investments automatically, helping you stay on top of your financial goals.

5. Practice Mindfulness: Develop mindfulness techniques to manage emotions and reduce impulsive decision-making.

- Example: Practice mindfulness meditation to stay calm and focused, especially during periods of market volatility.

Conclusion

Cognitive biases are inherent in human decision-making and can significantly impact financial behavior. By understanding these biases and implementing strategies to mitigate their effects, individuals can make more rational and informed financial decisions. Recognizing cognitive biases, developing structured decision-making processes, and leveraging technology and professional advice are crucial steps toward overcoming these biases. This chapter has explored common cognitive biases in the context of the psychology of money, their impact on financial behavior, and practical strategies for mitigating their effects. By applying these insights, individuals can enhance their financial well-being and achieve greater financial success.

CHAPTER 04

MONEY AND EMOTIONS

Money and emotions are intricately linked, with our financial decisions often being influenced by our emotional states. Understanding how emotions affect our financial behavior is crucial for making sound financial decisions and achieving long-term financial stability. This chapter explores the complex relationship between money and emotions, examining how different emotions such as fear, greed, joy, and stress influence financial behavior. It also provides strategies for managing emotions to improve financial decision-making and overall financial well-being.

The Relationship Between Money and Emotions

Emotions play a pivotal role in shaping our attitudes and behaviors toward money. Positive emotions can lead to impulsive spending and overconfidence in investments, while negative emotions can result in financial avoidance or overly conservative financial strategies. Recognizing the emotional drivers behind financial decisions is the first step toward achieving better financial outcomes.

Emotional Triggers in Financial Behavior

1. Fear: Fear of financial loss can lead to risk-averse behavior, such as avoiding investments or hoarding cash. Fear can also cause panic selling during market downturns.

2. Greed: The desire for wealth can drive individuals to take excessive risks in pursuit of high returns, often leading to speculative investments and overleveraging.

3. Joy and Excitement: Positive emotions can lead to impulsive spending and overconfidence in financial decisions, such as making large purchases or risky investments without adequate research.

4. Stress and Anxiety: Financial stress can cause avoidance of financial responsibilities, hasty decisions, or reliance on unhealthy coping mechanisms like retail therapy.

Fear and Financial Behavior

Fear is a powerful emotion that can significantly impact financial decisions. It often leads to risk-averse behavior and can prevent individuals from making necessary financial moves.

Manifestations of Fear in Financial Behavior

1. Avoidance of Investment: Fear of losing money can result in a reluctance to invest, causing individuals to miss out on potential growth opportunities.

2. Hoarding Cash: Fear of market volatility can lead to excessive cash reserves, which may not keep pace with inflation.

3. Financial Procrastination: Fear of making financial mistakes can lead to procrastination and avoidance of important financial tasks.

Example: During an economic downturn, fear might cause an individual to withdraw from the stock market and keep their money in a low-interest savings account, missing out on potential recovery gains.

Strategies to Manage Fear

1. Education and Research: Increase your financial knowledge to reduce uncertainty and build confidence in your decisions.

- Example: Take a course on investment basics to understand different asset classes and their risk profiles.

2. Diversification: Spread investments across various asset classes to mitigate risk and reduce fear of loss.

- Example: Create a diversified portfolio that includes stocks, bonds, and real estate to balance risk and reward.

3. Consult with Advisors: Seek professional financial advice to make informed decisions and alleviate fears.

- Example: Work with a financial advisor to develop a long-term investment strategy that aligns with your risk tolerance.

Greed and Financial Behavior

Greed, or the excessive desire for wealth, can drive individuals to take on significant risks in pursuit of high returns. It often leads to speculative investments and short-term thinking.

Manifestations of Greed in Financial Behavior

1. Speculative Investments: Greed can lead to investing in high-risk, high-reward opportunities without thorough research.

2. Overleveraging: The desire for quick profits can result in borrowing excessively to invest, increasing financial vulnerability.

3. Chasing Trends: Greed can cause individuals to follow investment fads, often buying high and selling low.

Example: An investor might pour all their money into a speculative stock or cryptocurrency, driven by the hope of substantial returns, without considering the potential for significant loss.

Strategies to Manage Greed

1. Set Clear Goals: Define long-term financial goals to focus on sustainable growth rather than short-term gains.

- Example: Create a financial plan that prioritizes long-term wealth building, such as saving for retirement or buying a home.

2. Adopt a Long-Term Perspective: Focus on long-term investment strategies rather than short-term speculative gains.

- Example: Invest in a diversified portfolio of stocks and bonds, aiming for steady growth over time.

3. Implement Risk Management: Use risk management techniques to limit exposure to high-risk investments.

- Example: Set limits on the amount of money allocated to speculative investments and use stop-loss orders to manage potential losses.

Joy, Excitement, and Financial Behavior

Positive emotions like joy and excitement can lead to impulsive spending and overconfidence in investment decisions. While these feelings can drive positive action, they can also result in financial mistakes if not managed properly.

Manifestations of Joy and Excitement in Financial Behavior

1. Impulsive Spending: Joy and excitement can lead to unplanned purchases and overspending on non-essential items.

2. Overconfidence in Investments: Positive emotions can result in overconfidence, leading to risky investment decisions based on optimism rather than analysis.

3. Short-Term Gratification: The pursuit of immediate pleasure can overshadow long-term financial planning and savings.

Example: After receiving a bonus, an individual might go on a shopping spree or invest in a trendy stock without conducting proper research, driven by the excitement of having extra money.

Strategies to Manage Joy and Excitement

1. Budgeting and Planning: Create a budget that includes discretionary spending limits to manage impulsive purchases.

- Example: Allocate a specific amount of your bonus for fun spending, while saving or investing the remainder.

2. Practice Mindfulness: Develop mindfulness techniques to stay grounded and make more rational decisions.

- Example: Practice mindfulness meditation to maintain focus and avoid impulsive financial decisions driven by excitement.

3. Stick to a Plan: Follow a structured financial plan to stay focused on long-term goals despite short-term emotions.

- Example: Refer to your financial plan when making decisions about spending or investing, ensuring alignment with your long-term objectives.

Stress and Financial Behavior

Money-related stress can lead to poor financial decision-making, such as avoiding financial responsibilities, making hasty decisions, or engaging in unhealthy coping mechanisms.

Manifestations of Stress in Financial Behavior

1. Financial Avoidance: Stress can lead to avoidance of financial tasks, such as budgeting, investing, or addressing debt.

2. Hasty Decisions: Stress can cause individuals to make quick, emotion-driven decisions without fully considering the consequences.

3. Unhealthy Coping Mechanisms: Stress may lead to behaviors like retail therapy, where spending is used as a way to alleviate emotional distress.

Example: An individual stressed about mounting credit card debt might avoid looking at their statements, leading to missed payments and increased interest charges.

Strategies to Manage Stress

1. Financial Planning: Develop a comprehensive financial plan to provide structure and reduce uncertainty.

- Example: Work with a financial advisor to create a plan that addresses debt management, savings, and investment goals.

2. Stress-Reduction Techniques: Practice stress-reduction techniques, such as exercise, meditation, and deep breathing, to manage anxiety.

- Example: Incorporate regular exercise and mindfulness practices into your routine to alleviate financial stress.

3. Seek Support: Engage with financial advisors, support groups, or therapists to address financial stress and develop healthy coping mechanisms.

- Example: Join a financial literacy group to share experiences and gain support from others facing similar financial challenges.

Integrating Emotional Management into Financial Planning

Effectively managing emotions is crucial for making sound financial decisions. By integrating emotional management strategies into financial planning, individuals can improve their financial behavior and outcomes.

Developing Emotional Awareness

Recognize and understand your emotions and how they influence your financial decisions. This awareness is the first step toward managing emotional responses effectively.

Example: Keep a journal of your financial decisions and the emotions you felt at the time. Reflect on how these emotions influenced your choices.

Setting Clear Financial Goals

Having clear financial goals provides a framework for decision-making and helps you stay focused on long-term objectives rather than short-term emotional reactions.

Example: Write down your financial goals, such as saving for a home or retirement, and create a plan to achieve them. Refer to this plan during periods of market volatility.

Practicing Mindfulness and Stress Reduction

Mindfulness and stress-reduction techniques, such as meditation and deep breathing exercises, can help manage emotional reactions to financial situations.

Example: Practice mindfulness meditation for a few minutes each day to stay calm and focused, especially during periods of financial uncertainty.

Creating and Following a Budget

A well-defined budget helps manage spending and ensures that financial decisions align with your goals and values, reducing the impact of impulsive emotional spending.

Example: Use a budgeting app to track your income and expenses, setting limits on discretionary spending to avoid impulsive purchases.

Consulting with Financial Advisors

Financial advisors can provide an objective perspective and help you make decisions based on logic and analysis rather than emotions.

Example: Schedule regular meetings with a financial advisor to review your financial plan and make adjustments as needed, especially during times of emotional stress.

Conclusion

Emotions such as fear, greed, joy, and stress significantly influence financial decisions and behaviors. Understanding how these feelings impact financial behavior is essential for making more informed and effective financial choices. By recognizing the psychological mechanisms underlying emotional responses and implementing strategies to manage emotions effectively, individuals can improve their financial behavior and achieve greater financial well-being. This chapter has explored how money and emotions are intertwined, providing insights and practical strategies for managing emotions in financial decision-making. By applying these strategies, individuals can navigate their financial journey with greater confidence and resilience.

CHAPTER 05

MONEY AND HAPPINESS

The relationship between money and happiness is complex and multifaceted. While money can provide comfort, security, and opportunities, it does not guarantee happiness. Understanding how money influences happiness and recognizing the limits of this influence can help individuals make better financial decisions that enhance their well-being. This chapter explores the connection between money and happiness, examining how financial stability, spending habits, and personal values impact overall life satisfaction. It also provides practical strategies for using money to improve happiness and well-being.

The Connection Between Money and Happiness

Money plays a significant role in our lives, and its influence on happiness is undeniable. However, the relationship between money and happiness is not straightforward. Several factors determine how money affects our well-being.

Financial Stability and Happiness

Financial stability is a crucial component of happiness. When individuals have enough money to meet their basic needs and feel secure about their financial future, they are more likely to experience higher levels of happiness.

Key Points:

- Basic Needs: Ensuring that basic needs such as food, shelter, and healthcare are met is fundamental to well-being.

- Security: Having a financial safety net, such as savings or insurance, reduces stress and anxiety about unexpected expenses.

- Debt Management: Managing and reducing debt can significantly improve financial stability and, consequently, happiness.

Example: A person with stable employment, a solid emergency fund, and manageable debt levels is likely to experience less financial stress and greater overall happiness.

Spending Habits and Happiness

How individuals spend their money can have a profound impact on their happiness. Certain spending habits are more likely to enhance well-being than others.

Key Points:

- Experiential Purchases: Spending money on experiences, such as travel, concerts, or dining out, tends to bring more happiness than purchasing material goods. Experiences create lasting memories and often involve social interactions.

- Giving to Others: Acts of generosity, such as donating to charity or buying gifts for loved ones, can boost happiness. Giving fosters a sense of connection and purpose.

- Investing in Health and Education: Spending on health and personal development can lead to long-term happiness by improving overall quality of life and providing a sense of achievement.

Example: Investing in a memorable family vacation is likely to bring more lasting happiness than buying a new television.

Personal Values and Happiness

Aligning financial decisions with personal values and goals can enhance happiness. When individuals use their money in ways that reflect their priorities and beliefs, they are more likely to feel fulfilled and content.

Key Points:

- Authenticity: Spending in ways that reflect one's true self and values leads to greater satisfaction.

- Purpose: Using money to achieve personal goals or contribute to causes one cares about provides a sense of purpose and fulfillment.

- Balance: Balancing spending on necessary expenses, personal enjoyment, and long-term goals ensures a well-rounded approach to financial well-being.

Example: A person who values education might find happiness in investing in courses or learning opportunities that align with their interests and career goals.

The Limits of Money's Influence on Happiness

While money can contribute to happiness, it has its limits. Beyond a certain point, increases in income have a diminishing impact on well-being. Understanding these limits can help individuals focus on what truly matters.

The Diminishing Returns of Income

Research shows that after reaching a certain level of income, additional wealth has a reduced impact on happiness. This phenomenon is known as the "diminishing returns" of income.

Key Points:

- Income Threshold: Studies suggest that once basic needs and moderate comforts are met, additional income contributes less to overall happiness.

- Relative Wealth: People often compare their wealth to others, which can affect happiness. The perception of being wealthier or poorer than peers can influence satisfaction more than absolute income levels.

Example: A person earning enough to live comfortably may not experience a significant increase in happiness by doubling their income, especially if they are already meeting their basic needs and enjoying some luxuries.

The Hedonic Treadmill

The "hedonic treadmill" is a concept that describes how individuals quickly adapt to changes in their financial situation. Over time, the happiness gained from financial improvements tends to fade, and people return to their baseline level of happiness.

Key Points:

- Adaptation: People tend to adapt to both positive and negative changes in their financial circumstances, which means that the initial happiness from a financial windfall can diminish over time.

- Pursuing More: Constantly striving for more wealth can lead to a cycle of perpetual dissatisfaction, as each new level of wealth becomes the new norm.

Example: After receiving a significant raise, an individual might feel happier initially, but over time, they may adapt to their new income level and no longer feel the same boost in happiness.

Strategies for Using Money to Enhance Happiness

Understanding how money influences happiness allows individuals to make more intentional financial decisions that promote well-being. Here are some strategies for using money to enhance happiness:

Focus on Financial Security

Ensuring financial security is a fundamental step toward happiness. Building a solid financial foundation reduces stress and provides peace of mind.

Steps to Take:

- Build an Emergency Fund: Save enough to cover three to six months' worth of living expenses in case of unexpected events.

- Reduce and Manage Debt: Pay down high-interest debt and avoid taking on unnecessary debt.

- Plan for the Future: Invest in retirement accounts and other long-term savings to secure your financial future.

Example: A person with a well-funded emergency savings account and a manageable debt load is likely to experience less financial stress and more peace of mind.

Spend on Experiences

Investing in experiences rather than material goods can lead to greater and longer-lasting happiness.

Steps to Take:

- Prioritize Experiences: Allocate a portion of your budget to activities and experiences that bring joy, such as travel, hobbies, and social events.

- Create Memories: Focus on experiences that create lasting memories and opportunities for connection with others.

Example: Instead of buying the latest gadget, consider taking a weekend getaway or attending a concert with friends.

Practice Generosity

Giving to others can boost happiness and create a sense of fulfillment and purpose.

Steps to Take:

- Donate to Causes: Support charities and organizations that align with your values and make a difference in areas you care about.

- Give Gifts: Spend money on thoughtful gifts for friends and family to strengthen relationships and spread joy.

Example: Making regular donations to a favorite charity or surprising a loved one with a meaningful gift can enhance your sense of well-being.

Invest in Health and Personal Growth

Spending on health and personal development can improve overall quality of life and contribute to long-term happiness.

Steps to Take:

- Health Investments: Prioritize spending on healthcare, fitness, and wellness activities that promote physical and mental health.

- Educational Opportunities: Invest in courses, books, and learning experiences that support personal and professional growth.

Example: Joining a fitness class or enrolling in a professional development course can lead to improved health and a greater sense of accomplishment.

Align Spending with Values

Ensure that your financial decisions reflect your personal values and long-term goals to enhance satisfaction and fulfillment.

Steps to Take:

- Identify Values: Reflect on what matters most to you and ensure your spending aligns with these values.

- Set Financial Goals: Establish clear, value-driven financial goals and create a plan to achieve them.

Example: If sustainability is important to you, consider investing in eco-friendly products and supporting businesses that prioritize environmental responsibility.

Conclusion

The relationship between money and happiness is complex, but understanding how money influences well-being can help individuals make more intentional financial decisions. Financial stability, thoughtful spending, and aligning financial decisions with personal values are key factors in using money to enhance happiness. By focusing on these areas and recognizing the limits of money's influence on happiness, individuals can improve their financial well-being and overall life satisfaction. This chapter has explored the connection between money and happiness, providing insights and practical strategies for using money to create a more fulfilling and joyful life.

CHAPTER 06

EMOTIONS IN THE PSYCHOLOGY OF FINANCE

Emotions play a pivotal role in financial decision-making. While traditional economic theories often assume that individuals are rational actors, real-world behavior frequently deviates from this ideal due to the influence of emotions. Understanding how emotions affect financial decisions is crucial for investors, financial professionals, and policymakers. This chapter explores the impact of various emotions on financial behavior and provides strategies for managing emotional influences to improve financial outcomes.

The Role of Emotions in Financial Decision-Making

Financial decisions are often made under conditions of uncertainty and risk, which can trigger strong emotional responses. Emotions such as fear, greed, excitement, and regret can significantly influence how individuals perceive risk and make financial choices. These emotional reactions can lead to irrational behaviors that deviate from optimal decision-making.

Fear

Fear is a powerful emotion that can lead to risk-averse behavior. In the context of finance, fear often manifests as a reluctance to invest or a tendency to sell assets during market downturns to avoid further losses. This can result in missed opportunities for gains and suboptimal investment performance.

Example: During the 2008 financial crisis, many investors panicked and sold their stocks at a loss, fearing further declines. This widespread selling exacerbated the market downturn and led to significant financial losses for many individuals.

Greed

Greed, or the desire for wealth and profit, can drive risk-seeking behavior and speculative investment. While a certain level of ambition is necessary for financial growth, excessive greed can lead to irrational decision-making and bubbles in asset prices.

Example: The dot-com bubble of the late 1990s was fueled by investor greed, as individuals poured money into internet companies with little regard for their fundamental value. The subsequent market crash left many investors with substantial losses.

Excitement

Excitement and optimism can influence financial decisions by leading individuals to take on more risk than they might otherwise consider. Positive emotions can create a sense of overconfidence, causing investors to underestimate potential downsides.

Example: During a bull market, widespread excitement and optimism can drive asset prices higher as investors become more willing to take on risk. This can lead to inflated valuations and eventual market corrections.

Regret

Regret is the emotion experienced when individuals realize that their decisions have led to undesirable outcomes. In finance, regret can lead to an aversion to making future decisions for fear of repeating past mistakes. This can result in overly cautious behavior and missed investment opportunities.

Example: An investor who experiences regret after a significant loss may become overly conservative in their future investment choices, avoiding potentially profitable opportunities due to fear of making another mistake.

Emotional Intelligence and Financial Decision-Making

Emotional intelligence, the ability to recognize and manage one's emotions, is a valuable skill in finance. Individuals with high emotional intelligence are better equipped to handle the emotional challenges of investing and can make more rational decisions. Developing emotional intelligence involves several key components:

- Self-awareness: Recognizing one's emotional state and understanding how it influences decision-making.

- Self-regulation: Managing emotions to prevent them from leading to impulsive or irrational decisions.

- Motivation: Using emotions constructively to drive financial goals and objectives.

- Empathy: Understanding the emotions of others, which can be useful in negotiations and collaborative financial decisions.

- Social skills: Building strong relationships and networks that can provide support and diverse perspectives in financial decision-making.

Strategies for Managing Emotions in Finance

While it is impossible to eliminate emotions from financial decision-making, there are strategies that can help individuals manage their emotional responses and make more rational choices:

Establishing a Plan

Having a clear financial plan and investment strategy can provide a framework for decision-making, reducing the influence of emotions. A well-defined plan can help individuals stay focused on their long-term goals and avoid making impulsive decisions based on short-term market fluctuations.

Example: An investor with a diversified portfolio and a clear investment horizon is less likely to panic during market downturns, as they have a plan in place to weather short-term volatility.

Setting Limits

Setting predefined limits on investment decisions, such as stop-loss orders or maximum position sizes, can help mitigate the impact of emotions. These limits can act as safeguards, preventing individuals from making overly emotional decisions during periods of market stress.

Example: A stop-loss order automatically sells security when its price falls below a certain level, helping investors avoid large losses driven by emotional responses to market declines.

Practicing Mindfulness

Mindfulness techniques, such as meditation and deep breathing exercises, can help individuals manage stress and maintain emotional balance. Practicing mindfulness can improve emotional regulation and enhance decision-making under pressure.

Example: An investor who practices mindfulness may be better able to stay calm and focused during periods of market volatility, making more rational and measured decisions.

Seeking Professional Advice

Consulting with financial advisors or other professionals can provide an objective perspective and help counteract emotional biases. Advisors can offer guidance based on experience and expertise, helping individuals make informed decisions.

Example: A financial advisor can help an investor stay disciplined and focused on their long-term goals, even when emotions run high during market downturns or periods of exuberance.

The Impact of Collective Emotions on Financial Markets

Emotions do not only influence individual investors; they also have a significant impact on collective market behavior. When emotions are shared among a large number of investors, they can drive market trends and create feedback loops that amplify price movements.

Market Bubbles

Market bubbles occur when asset prices are driven to unsustainable levels by collective investor enthusiasm and greed. Bubbles are often characterized by rapid price increases, speculative trading, and a disregard for fundamental valuations.

Example: The housing bubble of the mid-2000s was fueled by widespread optimism about rising home prices, leading to excessive borrowing and investment in real estate. The subsequent burst of the bubble led to the 2008 financial crisis.

Market Crashes

Market crashes happen when fear and panic spread among investors, leading to rapid sell-offs and sharp declines in asset prices. Crashes are often triggered by negative news or events that undermine investor confidence.

Example: The stock market crash of 1987, known as Black Monday, was driven by panic selling and a loss of confidence among investors, resulting in a dramatic decline in stock prices.

Conclusion

Emotions play a crucial role in financial decision-making, influencing how individuals perceive risk, make investment choices, and react to market events. Understanding the impact of emotions such as fear, greed, excitement, and regret is essential for making more rational and informed financial decisions. By developing emotional intelligence and adopting strategies to manage emotional responses, individuals can improve their financial outcomes and navigate the complexities of the financial markets with greater confidence and stability. This chapter has explored the key emotional factors that affect financial behavior, providing a foundation for further exploration of psychological principles in finance.

CHAPTER 07

EMOTIONS IN THE PSYCHOLOGY OF MONEY

Emotions play a critical role in how individuals perceive and manage their money. The psychology of money examines how feelings such as fear, greed, joy, and stress influence financial decisions and behaviors. Understanding the emotional aspects of money can help individuals make more rational financial choices and improve their overall financial well-being. This chapter explores the impact of various emotions on financial behavior, the underlying psychological mechanisms, and strategies for managing emotions in financial decision-making.

The Role of Emotions in Financial Behavior

Emotions can significantly impact financial decisions and behavior. Positive emotions like joy and excitement can lead to impulsive spending, while negative emotions like fear and stress can result in overly conservative financial strategies or avoidance of financial responsibilities.

Fear

Fear is a powerful emotion that can lead to risk-averse behavior. In the context of money, fear often manifests as a reluctance to invest, a tendency to hoard cash, or anxiety about financial security.

Impact on Financial Behavior:

- Risk Aversion: Fear can cause individuals to avoid investments perceived as risky, potentially missing out on higher returns.

- Hoarding Cash: Fear of market volatility can lead to keeping excessive cash reserves, which may not keep pace with inflation.

- Financial Avoidance: Fear of making financial mistakes can lead to procrastination or avoidance of financial planning.

Example: During an economic downturn, an individual might withdraw money from the stock market and keep it in a low-yield savings account, driven by fear of further losses.

Greed

Greed, or the excessive desire for wealth, can drive individuals to take on excessive risks in pursuit of high returns. It can lead to speculative investments and overleveraging.

Impact on Financial Behavior:

- Speculative Investments: Greed can drive individuals to invest in high-risk, high-reward opportunities without adequate research.

- Overleveraging: The desire for quick profits can lead to borrowing excessively to invest, increasing financial vulnerability.

- Short-Term Focus: Greed often leads to a focus on short-term gains at the expense of long-term financial stability.

Example: An investor might put all their savings into a speculative stock or cryptocurrency, hoping for a substantial return, without considering the risks.

Joy and Excitement

Positive emotions like joy and excitement can influence financial behavior by encouraging spending and investment decisions based on emotional highs rather than rational analysis.

Impact on Financial Behavior:

- Impulsive Spending: Joy and excitement can lead to impulsive purchases and overspending on non-essential items.

- Overconfidence in Investments: Positive emotions can result in overconfidence, leading to risky investment decisions based on optimism rather than fundamentals.

Example: After receiving a bonus, an individual might go on a shopping spree or invest in a trendy stock without proper research, driven by the excitement of having extra money.

Stress and Anxiety

Stress and anxiety about money can lead to poor financial decision-making, such as avoiding financial planning, making hasty decisions, or engaging in unhealthy coping mechanisms.

Impact on Financial Behavior:

- Financial Avoidance: Anxiety can lead to avoidance of financial tasks, such as budgeting, investing, or addressing debt.

- Hasty Decisions: Stress can cause individuals to make quick, emotion-driven decisions without fully considering the consequences.

- Unhealthy Coping Mechanisms: Stress may lead to behaviors like retail therapy, where spending is used as a way to alleviate emotional distress.

Example: An individual stressed about mounting credit card debt might avoid looking at their statements, leading to missed payments and increased interest charges.

Psychological Mechanisms Underlying Emotional Responses

Understanding the psychological mechanisms that underlie emotional responses to money can provide insights into how to manage these emotions effectively.

Cognitive Appraisal

Cognitive appraisal refers to the process by which individuals evaluate and interpret financial situations, influencing their emotional responses. How a person appraises a financial event can determine whether they experience it as stressful, exciting, or inconsequential.

Example: Two individuals might receive the same financial news, such as a stock market decline. One might appraise it as a temporary setback and remain calm, while the other might see it as a financial disaster and panic.

Emotional Regulation

Emotional regulation involves managing and responding to emotional experiences in a healthy and productive way. Effective emotional regulation can help individuals make more rational financial decisions.

Example: Practicing mindfulness and stress-reduction techniques can help individuals stay calm during financial uncertainty and make better decisions.

Behavioral Economics

Behavioral economics studies how psychological factors, including emotions, affect economic decision-making. It highlights the influence of irrational behaviors driven by emotional responses, such as overconfidence and loss aversion.

Example: Understanding behavioral economics can help individuals recognize when emotions like fear or greed are driving their decisions, allowing them to take a step back and assess the situation more rationally.

Strategies for Managing Emotions in Financial Decision-Making

Managing emotions is crucial for making sound financial decisions. Here are strategies to help individuals manage their emotions and improve their financial behavior:

1. Develop Emotional Awareness

Recognize and understand your emotions and how they influence your financial decisions. This awareness is the first step toward managing emotional responses effectively.

Example: Keep a journal of your financial decisions and the emotions you felt at the time. Reflect on how these emotions influenced your choices.

2. Practice Mindfulness and Stress Reduction

Mindfulness and stress-reduction techniques, such as meditation and deep breathing exercises, can help manage emotional reactions to financial situations.

Example: Practice mindfulness meditation for a few minutes each day to stay calm and focused, especially during periods of financial uncertainty.

3. Set Clear Financial Goals

Having clear financial goals provides a framework for decision-making and helps you stay focused on long-term objectives rather than short-term emotional reactions.

Example: Write down your financial goals, such as saving for a home or retirement, and create a plan to achieve them. Refer to this plan during periods of market volatility.

4. Create and Follow a Budget

A well-defined budget helps manage spending and ensures that financial decisions align with your goals and values, reducing the impact of impulsive emotional spending.

Example: Use a budgeting app to track your income and expenses, setting limits on discretionary spending to avoid impulsive purchases.

5. Consult with Financial Advisors

Financial advisors can provide an objective perspective and help you make decisions based on logic and analysis rather than emotions.

Example: Schedule regular meetings with a financial advisor to review your financial plan and make adjustments as needed, especially during times of emotional stress.

6. Diversify Investments

Diversifying investments can help manage risk and reduce anxiety about market fluctuations, providing a more stable financial foundation.

Example: Invest in a mix of asset classes, such as stocks, bonds, and real estate, to spread risk and reduce the emotional impact of market volatility.

Conclusion

Emotions play a significant role in financial behavior, influencing how individuals perceive and manage their money. Understanding the impact of emotions such as fear, greed, joy, and stress on financial decisions is crucial for making more rational and informed choices. By recognizing the psychological mechanisms underlying emotional responses and implementing strategies to manage emotions effectively, individuals can improve their financial behavior and achieve greater financial well-being. This chapter has explored the role of emotions in the psychology of money, providing insights and practical strategies for managing emotions in financial decision-making. By applying these strategies, individuals can navigate their financial journey with greater confidence and resilience.

CHAPTER 08

FINANCIAL STREE AND MENTAL HEALTH

Financial stress is a prevalent issue that can significantly impact mental health. Concerns about money can lead to anxiety, depression, and other mental health issues, affecting overall well-being and quality of life. Understanding the relationship between financial stress and mental health is crucial for developing effective coping strategies and achieving financial stability. This chapter explores the causes and effects of financial stress, examines its impact on mental health, and provides practical strategies for managing financial stress to improve mental well-being.

Understanding Financial Stress

Financial stress arises from various financial pressures, such as debt, unexpected expenses, job loss, and insufficient savings. It is a state of worry, anxiety, or unease related to money and financial matters.

Common Causes of Financial Stress

1. Debt: High levels of debt, such as credit card debt, student loans, and mortgages, can create ongoing financial pressure and anxiety.

2. Unexpected Expenses: Unforeseen costs, such as medical bills, car repairs, or home maintenance, can strain finances and cause stress.

3. Income Instability: Irregular income or job loss can lead to uncertainty and financial insecurity.

4. Insufficient Savings: Lack of savings for emergencies or future goals can lead to a constant sense of financial vulnerability.

5. High Cost of Living: Rising costs of living, including housing, healthcare, and education, can outpace income growth, leading to financial strain.

Example: An individual with significant credit card debt and no emergency savings may experience chronic financial stress, leading to anxiety and difficulty concentrating on daily tasks.

The Impact of Financial Stress on Mental Health

Financial stress can have profound effects on mental health, contributing to a range of emotional and psychological issues.

Anxiety

Financial stress is a common trigger for anxiety, characterized by excessive worry and fear about financial matters.

Symptoms of Anxiety:

- Persistent worry about money

- Restlessness and irritability

- Difficulty concentrating

- Sleep disturbances

Example: An individual may lie awake at night, worrying about how to pay upcoming bills or manage debt, leading to chronic sleep problems and heightened anxiety during the day.

Depression

Prolonged financial stress can lead to depression, a mood disorder characterized by persistent feelings of sadness, hopelessness, and loss of interest in activities.

Symptoms of Depression:

- Feelings of sadness and hopelessness

- Loss of interest in activities once enjoyed

- Fatigue and low energy

- Changes in appetite and sleep patterns

- Difficulty concentrating and making decisions

Example: A person overwhelmed by financial difficulties may withdraw from social activities, lose interest in hobbies, and feel unable to cope with daily responsibilities.

Other Mental Health Issues

Financial stress can also contribute to other mental health issues, such as substance abuse, relationship problems, and decreased self-esteem.

Symptoms and Consequences:

- Substance Abuse: Some individuals may turn to alcohol or drugs as a coping mechanism for financial stress.

- Relationship Problems: Financial stress can strain relationships, leading to conflicts and reduced emotional support.

- Decreased Self-Esteem: Persistent financial struggles can erode self-esteem and lead to feelings of inadequacy and failure.

Example: A person experiencing financial stress may argue frequently with their partner about money, leading to relationship strain and decreased emotional well-being.

Strategies for Managing Financial Stress

Effective management of financial stress involves addressing both the financial issues and the emotional responses associated with them. Here are practical strategies for managing financial stress and improving mental health:

1. Develop a Financial Plan

Creating a comprehensive financial plan can provide structure and reduce uncertainty, helping to alleviate financial stress.

Steps to Take:

- Assess Your Financial Situation: Take stock of your income, expenses, debts, and savings to understand your current financial position.

- Set Financial Goals: Define short-term and long-term financial goals, such as paying off debt, building an emergency fund, and saving for retirement.

- Create a Budget: Develop a realistic budget that aligns with your financial goals and tracks income and expenses.

- Monitor Progress: Regularly review your financial plan and adjust as needed to stay on track.

Example: An individual with significant debt might create a debt repayment plan, prioritize payments, and track progress to reduce financial stress and regain control over their finances.

2. Build an Emergency Fund

An emergency fund provides a financial safety net for unexpected expenses, reducing the stress associated with financial emergencies.

Steps to Take:

- Start Small: Begin by setting aside a small amount each month, gradually increasing your savings over time.

- Automate Savings: Set up automatic transfers to a dedicated savings account to ensure consistent contributions.

- Aim for a Target: Aim to save three to six months' worth of living expenses to cover potential emergencies.

Example: A person with an emergency fund is less likely to experience financial stress when faced with unexpected car repairs or medical bills, as they have the resources to cover these expenses.

3. Seek Professional Advice

Financial advisors and counselors can provide expert guidance and support, helping you navigate financial challenges and develop effective strategies.

Steps to Take:

- Find a Financial Advisor: Look for a certified financial advisor who can help you create a financial plan and offer personalized advice.

- Consider Credit Counseling: If struggling with debt, consider working with a credit counselor to develop a debt management plan.

- Access Mental Health Services: If financial stress is affecting your mental health, seek support from a therapist or counselor.

Example: An individual overwhelmed by debt might work with a credit counselor to negotiate with creditors and develop a manageable repayment plan, reducing financial stress and improving mental health.

4. Practice Stress-Reduction Techniques

Incorporating stress-reduction techniques into your daily routine can help manage the emotional impact of financial stress.

Steps to Take:

- Exercise Regularly: Physical activity can reduce stress, improve mood, and boost overall well-being.

- Practice Mindfulness: Mindfulness techniques, such as meditation and deep breathing exercises, can help calm the mind and reduce anxiety.

- Prioritize Sleep: Ensure you get adequate sleep each night to support your mental and physical health.

Example: Practicing mindfulness meditation for a few minutes each day can help an individual manage financial stress and maintain a sense of calm and focus.

5. Foster Supportive Relationships

Building a network of supportive friends, family, or financial mentors can provide emotional support and practical advice.

Steps to Take:

- Communicate Openly: Share your financial concerns with trusted friends or family members who can offer support and understanding.

- Join Support Groups: Consider joining financial literacy or support groups where you can share experiences and gain insights from others facing similar challenges.

- Seek Professional Support: Engage with financial advisors or mental health professionals for additional guidance and support.

Example: Joining a financial support group can help an individual feel less isolated in their financial struggles, gain new perspectives, and receive encouragement from others.

Conclusion

Financial stress is a common issue that can significantly impact mental health. By understanding the relationship between financial stress and mental health, individuals can develop effective coping strategies to manage financial pressures and improve their overall well-being. This chapter has explored the causes and effects of financial stress, examined its impact on mental health, and provided practical strategies for managing financial stress. By creating a financial plan, building an emergency fund, seeking professional advice, practicing stress-reduction techniques, and fostering supportive relationships, individuals can reduce financial stress and enhance their mental health and overall quality of life.

CHAPTER 09

MINDFULNESS IN MONEY MANAGEMENT

Mindfulness, the practice of being fully present and engaged in the current moment, can significantly improve money management. By incorporating mindfulness into financial practices, individuals can enhance their financial decision-making, reduce stress, and achieve greater financial stability and well-being. This chapter explores the concept of mindfulness in money management, its benefits, and practical strategies for applying mindfulness to various aspects of financial life.

Understanding Mindfulness

Mindfulness involves paying attention to the present moment without judgment. It is about being aware of your thoughts, feelings, and surroundings, and accepting them as they are. This practice can help individuals become more aware of their financial habits and make more intentional financial decisions.

Key Components of Mindfulness

1. Awareness: Being conscious of your thoughts, emotions, and behaviors in the present moment.

2. Non-Judgment: Observing your experiences without labeling them as good or bad.

3. Acceptance: Acknowledging your thoughts and feelings without trying to change them immediately.

Example: Practicing mindfulness while reviewing your budget can help you understand your spending habits and emotional triggers without feeling overwhelmed or guilty.

Benefits of Mindfulness in Money Management

Incorporating mindfulness into money management can lead to several benefits, including improved financial decision-making, reduced financial stress, and enhanced overall well-being.

Improved Financial Decision-Making

Mindfulness can help individuals make more rational and informed financial decisions by increasing awareness of their financial habits and emotional triggers.

Key Points:

- Clarity: Mindfulness provides clarity and focus, enabling individuals to evaluate financial decisions more objectively.

- Intentionality: Mindful individuals are more likely to make intentional financial choices that align with their values and goals.

Example: By practicing mindfulness, a person might recognize that they tend to make impulsive purchases when stressed and develop strategies to manage stress without overspending.

Reduced Financial Stress

Mindfulness can reduce financial stress by promoting a calm and balanced approach to financial challenges.

Key Points:

- Stress Reduction: Mindfulness techniques, such as deep breathing and meditation, can reduce anxiety and stress related to financial issues.

- Emotional Regulation: Mindfulness helps individuals regulate their emotions, preventing impulsive financial decisions driven by fear or excitement.

Example: A person who practices mindfulness might approach a financial setback, such as an unexpected expense, with a calm and measured response rather than panic.

Enhanced Overall Well-Being

Mindfulness contributes to overall well-being by fostering a positive and balanced relationship with money.

Key Points:

- Balance: Mindfulness encourages a balanced approach to spending, saving, and investing, promoting long-term financial health.

- Satisfaction: Mindful individuals are more likely to experience satisfaction and contentment with their financial situation, regardless of their income level.

Example: Practicing mindfulness can help an individual appreciate the financial resources they have and focus on their financial goals without constantly striving for more.

Practical Strategies for Applying Mindfulness to Money Management

There are several practical strategies for incorporating mindfulness into various aspects of money management, including budgeting, spending, saving, and investing.

Mindful Budgeting

Creating and maintaining a budget is a fundamental aspect of money management. Applying mindfulness to budgeting can enhance its effectiveness and make the process more meaningful.

Steps to Take:

- Set Clear Intentions: Start by setting clear financial intentions and goals for your budget. Reflect on what you want to achieve and why.

- Example: Set an intention to save for a down payment on a home and understand why this goal is important to you.

- Track Expenses Mindfully: Track your expenses with full awareness, paying attention to how and why you spend money.

- Example: Review your daily expenses at the end of each day, noting any emotional triggers that led to unplanned purchases.

- Regular Reflection: Regularly review your budget and reflect on your spending and saving patterns. Adjust your budget as needed to stay aligned with your goals.

- Example: Set aside time each month to review your budget, reflect on your progress, and make any necessary adjustments.

Mindful Spending

Mindful spending involves being fully aware of your spending habits and making intentional choices that align with your values and financial goals.

Steps to Take:

- Pause Before Purchases: Before making a purchase, take a moment to pause and consider whether it aligns with your values and financial goals.

- Example: Before buying a new gadget, pause and ask yourself if it aligns with your long-term financial goals or if it's an impulsive purchase.

- Evaluate Needs vs. Wants: Differentiate between needs and wants, and prioritize spending on what truly matters.

- Example: Reflect on whether a purchase is a need or a want, and prioritize spending on essentials and meaningful experiences.

- Practice Gratitude: Practice gratitude for what you already have to reduce the urge for unnecessary purchases.

- Example: Keep a gratitude journal and regularly write down things you appreciate about your current financial situation and possessions.

Mindful Saving

Mindful saving involves being intentional about setting aside money for future needs and goals and finding satisfaction in the act of saving.

Steps to Take:

- Set Specific Goals: Set specific, achievable saving goals that align with your financial intentions and values.

- Example: Set a goal to save $5,000 for an emergency fund within the next year, and understand why this goal is important to your financial security.

- Automate Savings: Automate your savings to ensure consistent contributions and reduce the temptation to spend.

- Example: Set up automatic transfers to your savings account each month to ensure consistent progress toward your goals.

- Celebrate Progress: Regularly review your savings progress and celebrate milestones to stay motivated.

- Example: When you reach a savings milestone, such as saving $1,000, celebrate your achievement in a meaningful and mindful way.

Mindful Investing

Mindful investing involves making investment decisions with awareness and intentionality, focusing on long-term goals, and aligning investments with personal values.

Steps to Take:

- Research and Educate: Take the time to research and understand different investment options and their potential risks and rewards.

- Example: Educate yourself about different types of investments, such as stocks, bonds, and mutual funds, before making investment decisions.

- Align with Values: Choose investments that align with your personal values and long-term financial goals.

- Example: Consider socially responsible investments that align with your ethical values and contribute to positive social impact.

- Regular Review: Regularly review your investment portfolio and make adjustments as needed to stay aligned with your goals.

- Example: Set aside time each quarter to review your investment portfolio, assess its performance, and make any necessary adjustments.

Integrating Mindfulness into Daily Financial Practices

Incorporating mindfulness into daily financial practices can enhance overall financial well-being and promote a healthier relationship with money.

Daily Mindfulness Practices

1. Mindful Morning Routine: Start your day with a mindful morning routine that includes a few minutes of meditation or deep breathing to set a positive tone for the day.

- Example: Spend five minutes each morning practicing mindfulness meditation to cultivate a sense of calm and focus.

2. Mindful Spending Check-In: Before making any purchase, take a moment to pause and reflect on whether it aligns with your financial goals and values.

- Example: Before buying a coffee on your way to work, pause and consider whether it aligns with your financial priorities.

3. Gratitude Practice: Incorporate gratitude practice into your daily routine to appreciate your financial resources and reduce the urge for unnecessary spending.

- Example: Each evening, write down three things you are grateful for related to your financial situation.

Weekly Mindfulness Practices

1. Budget Review: Set aside time each week to review your budget, track your expenses, and reflect on your financial decisions.

- Example: Spend 30 minutes each Sunday reviewing your budget, tracking your expenses, and reflecting on your spending habits.

2. Financial Reflection: Reflect on your financial goals and progress, and make any necessary adjustments to stay on track.

- Example: Reflect on your financial goals each week and assess whether your current financial behaviors align with those goals.

Monthly Mindfulness Practices

1. Financial Health Check: Conduct a monthly financial health check to review your overall financial situation, including your savings, investments, and debt.

- Example: Review your bank statements, investment accounts, and debt balances each month to assess your overall financial health.

2. Mindful Goal Setting: Set or reassess your financial goals each month to ensure they remain aligned with your values and priorities.

- Example: Set or reassess your financial goals at the beginning of each month, considering any changes in your financial situation or priorities.

Conclusion

Mindfulness in money management involves being fully present and intentional in your financial decisions and practices. By incorporating mindfulness into budgeting, spending, saving, and investing, individuals can improve their financial decision-making, reduce stress, and achieve greater financial well-being. This chapter has explored the concept of mindfulness in money management, its benefits, and practical strategies for applying mindfulness to various aspects of financial life. By adopting these strategies and integrating mindfulness into daily, weekly, and monthly financial practices, individuals can cultivate a healthier relationship with money and enhance their overall financial health and well-being.

CHAPTER 10

SOCIAL INFLUENCES IN THE PSYCHOLOGY OF FINANCE

Human behavior is profoundly influenced by social factors. In the realm of finance, social influences play a significant role in shaping financial decisions and market dynamics. Understanding how social norms, peer pressure, and collective behavior affect financial choices is crucial for investors and financial professionals. This chapter explores the impact of social influences on financial behavior and provides strategies for managing these effects to make more informed and rational financial decisions.

The Role of Social Influences in Financial Decision-Making

Social influences refer to the effects that the actions, opinions, and behaviors of others have on an individual's decisions. In finance, social influences can manifest in various ways, such as herd behavior, peer pressure, and the impact of media and social networks. These influences can drive market trends, create bubbles, and lead to collective behaviors that deviate from fundamental values.

Herd Behavior

Herd behavior occurs when individuals mimic the actions of a larger group, often leading to market trends that are not based on fundamental values. Herd behavior can drive asset prices to unsustainable levels during market bubbles or lead to sharp declines during market crashes.

Example: During the cryptocurrency boom of 2017, many investors bought into Bitcoin and other cryptocurrencies because others were doing so, driving prices to record highs. The subsequent crash in 2018 led to significant losses for many of these investors.

Peer Pressure

Peer pressure is the influence exerted by a peer group on individuals to align their behavior with group norms and expectations. In finance, peer pressure can lead individuals to make investment decisions based on the actions or opinions of friends, family, or colleagues, rather than on independent analysis.

Example: An individual might invest in a particular stock because their friends or coworkers are doing so, even if they do not fully understand the stock's fundamentals or risks involved.

Media and Social Networks

Media and social networks play a significant role in shaping public perception and influencing financial decisions. News articles, social media posts, and financial influencers can all impact investor sentiment and drive market movements.

Example: A positive news article about a company can lead to a surge in its stock price as investors rush to buy shares. Conversely, negative media coverage can lead to a sharp decline in the stock's value.

The Impact of Social Influences on Financial Markets

Social influences not only affect individual investors but also have broader implications for financial markets. When many investors exhibit similar behaviors due to social influences, their collective actions can drive significant market trends and create feedback loops that amplify price movements.

Market Bubbles

Market bubbles occur when asset prices are driven to unsustainable levels by collective investor enthusiasm and herd behavior. Bubbles are often characterized by rapid price increases, speculative trading, and a disregard for fundamental valuations.

Example: The housing bubble of the mid-2000s was fueled by widespread optimism about rising home prices and peer pressure to invest in real estate. The subsequent burst of the bubble led to the 2008 financial crisis.

Market Crashes

Market crashes happen when fear and panic spread among investors, leading to rapid sell-offs and sharp declines in asset prices. Crashes are often triggered by negative news or events that undermine investor confidence.

Example: The stock market crash of 1987, known as Black Monday, was driven by panic selling and a loss of confidence among investors, resulting in a dramatic decline in stock prices.

Strategies for Managing Social Influences in Finance

While it is impossible to eliminate social influences from financial decision-making, there are strategies that can help individuals manage these effects and make more rational choices:

Independent Research and Analysis

Conducting independent research and analysis can help individuals make informed decisions based on fundamental values rather than social influences. By gathering and evaluating data from reliable sources, investors can form their own opinions and avoid being swayed by the actions of others.

Example: Before making an investment, an individual can analyze the company's financial statements, industry trends, and potential risks to make an informed decision rather than relying on the opinions of friends or media coverage.

Diversification

Diversifying investments can help reduce the impact of social influences on overall portfolio performance. By spreading investments across different asset classes and sectors, individuals can protect themselves from the effects of herd behavior and market volatility.

Example: An investor with a diversified portfolio is less likely to be significantly affected by a market crash in a single asset class, as their investments are spread across various sectors.

Setting Clear Investment Criteria

Establishing clear investment criteria and sticking to them can help individuals stay disciplined and focused on their long-term goals. This involves setting specific criteria for selecting investments, such as valuation metrics, growth potential, and risk tolerance.

Example: An investor might decide only to invest in companies with a price-to-earnings ratio below a certain threshold and a consistent history of revenue growth, regardless of market trends or social influences.

Seeking Professional Advice

Consulting with financial advisors or other professionals can provide an objective perspective and help counteract the influence of social factors. Advisors can offer guidance based on experience and expertise, helping individuals make informed decisions.

Example: A financial advisor can help an investor develop a long-term investment strategy and stay disciplined during periods of market volatility, providing reassurance and reducing the impact of social influences.

Conclusion

Social influences play a significant role in shaping financial behavior and market dynamics. By understanding the impact of herd behavior, peer pressure, and media influences, individuals can develop strategies to manage these effects and make more rational financial decisions. This chapter has explored the key social factors that affect financial decision-making, providing a foundation for further exploration of psychological principles in finance. By conducting independent research, diversifying investments, setting clear investment criteria, and seeking professional advice, individuals can navigate the complexities of the financial markets with greater confidence and stability.

87

CHAPTER 11

SOCIAL INFLUENCES IN THE PSYCHOLOGY OF MONEY

Human behavior is profoundly influenced by social factors, and financial decisions are no exception. Social influences such as norms, peer pressure, herd behavior, and the impact of media and social networks play significant roles in shaping how individuals approach money management and financial planning. Understanding these social influences is crucial for recognizing why people make certain financial choices and how these choices can affect broader financial outcomes. This chapter examines the impact of social influences on financial behavior and offers strategies for managing these influences to make more informed and rational financial decisions.

Social Norms and Financial Behavior

Social norms are the accepted behaviors and beliefs within a society or group. These norms can significantly influence financial decisions by establishing what is considered appropriate or desirable behavior.

Impact on Financial Behavior

Social norms can drive individuals to conform to the financial behaviors of their peers, even if those behaviors are not optimal. This can lead to decisions that are more about fitting in than about achieving the best financial outcomes.

Example: In a community where home ownership is highly valued, individuals might feel pressured to buy a house even if it is not the best financial decision for their situation, potentially leading to financial strain or debt.

Strategies for Managing Social Norms

1. Awareness and Education: Understanding the influence of social norms on financial decisions can help individuals make more informed choices based on personal financial goals rather than societal expectations.

   - Example: Reflect on your financial decisions and consider whether they are influenced by social norms or aligned with your financial goals.

2. Objective Financial Planning: Develop a financial plan based on objective criteria and personal goals, reducing the influence of social norms.

- Example: Create a budget and investment strategy that prioritize your long-term financial goals, regardless of societal pressures.

Peer Pressure and Financial Decisions

Peer pressure refers to the influence exerted by a peer group to encourage conformity to group behaviors and decisions. In finance, peer pressure can lead individuals to make investment choices based on what their friends, family, or colleagues are doing, rather than on their own research and analysis.

Impact on Financial Behavior

Peer pressure can result in individuals making investment decisions that they do not fully understand or that are not aligned with their risk tolerance and financial goals.

Example: An individual might invest in a particular stock or cryptocurrency because their friends are doing so, without conducting their own due diligence. This can lead to financial losses if the investment turns out to be risky or unsuitable.

Strategies for Managing Peer Pressure

1. Independent Research: Conduct independent research and analysis to make informed decisions based on your own financial situation and goals.

- Example: Before making an investment, thoroughly research the asset, its performance history, and potential risks.

2. Setting Personal Financial Goals: Establish clear financial goals and a strategy to achieve them, providing a framework for decision-making that is less influenced by peer pressure.

- Example: Define your financial objectives, such as retirement savings or buying a home, and create a plan to achieve them.

3. Consulting Professionals: Seek advice from financial advisors to gain an objective perspective and ensure that your investment decisions are aligned with your financial goals.

- Example: Schedule regular consultations with a financial advisor to review your investment strategy and make adjustments as needed.

Herd Behavior and Financial Markets

Herd behavior occurs when individuals mimic the actions of a larger group, often leading to market trends that are not based on fundamental values. This behavior can drive asset prices to unsustainable levels during market bubbles or lead to sharp declines during market crashes.

Impact on Financial Behavior

Herd behavior can lead to irrational investment decisions, as individuals follow the crowd without conducting their own analysis or considering the fundamentals.

Example: During the housing bubble of the mid-2000s, many people bought homes at inflated prices because everyone else was doing so. When the bubble burst, it led to significant financial losses and foreclosures.

Strategies for Managing Herd Behavior

1. Critical Thinking: Develop critical thinking skills to evaluate investments based on your own research and analysis rather than simply following the crowd.

   - Example: Analyze the fundamental value of an investment and consider its long-term potential before making a decision.

2. Diversification: Diversify investments to manage risk and reduce the impact of herd behavior on your overall portfolio performance.

   - Example: Invest in a mix of asset classes, such as stocks, bonds, and real estate, to minimize risk and maximize returns.

3. Long-Term Perspective: Focus on long-term financial goals rather than short-term market trends driven by herd behavior.

- Example: Stick to your long-term investment strategy during periods of market volatility, avoiding impulsive decisions based on short-term trends.

Media and Social Networks

Media and social networks play a significant role in shaping public perception and influencing financial decisions. News articles, social media posts, and financial influencers can all impact investor sentiment and drive market movements.

Impact of Media on Financial Behavior

The media can amplify market trends by highlighting certain events, stocks, or economic indicators, leading to increased investor attention and action.

Example: Positive news coverage about a company can lead to a surge in its stock price as investors rush to buy shares. Conversely, negative news can lead to sharp declines as investors sell off assets.

Impact of Social Networks on Financial Behavior

Social networks allow for rapid dissemination of information and can create echo chambers where certain viewpoints are reinforced. Financial decisions can be heavily influenced by the opinions and behaviors shared on these platforms.

Example: The GameStop short squeeze in early 2021 was largely driven by discussions and coordination among retail investors on social media platforms like Reddit. This collective action led to significant price volatility and market disruptions.

Strategies for Managing Media and Social Network Influence

1. Verify Information: Always verify information from multiple reliable sources before making investment decisions based on media or social network inputs.

   - Example: Cross-check news articles and social media posts with reputable financial news sources and official company announcements.

2. Limit Exposure: Limit exposure to financial news and social media to reduce the emotional impact of sensational headlines and trending topics.

   - Example: Set specific times to check financial news and social media, avoiding constant monitoring.

3. Focus on Fundamentals: Base investment decisions on fundamental analysis and long-term financial goals rather than short-term media hype or social media trends.

   - Example: Conduct a thorough analysis of a company's financial health, growth potential, and market position before investing.

Integrating Social Influence Management into Financial Planning

Effectively managing social influences is crucial for making sound financial decisions. By integrating strategies to manage social influences into financial planning, individuals can improve their financial behavior and outcomes.

Developing Social Awareness

Recognize and understand how social influences impact your financial decisions. This awareness is the first step toward managing these influences effectively.

Example: Reflect on past financial decisions and identify whether they were influenced by social norms, peer pressure, or media coverage.

Setting Clear Financial Goals

Having clear financial goals provides a framework for decision-making and helps you stay focused on long-term objectives rather than short-term social influences.

Example: Write down your financial goals, such as saving for a home or retirement, and create a plan to achieve them. Refer to this plan when making financial decisions.

Seeking Professional Advice

Financial advisors can provide an objective perspective and help you make decisions based on logic and analysis rather than social influences.

Example: Schedule regular meetings with a financial advisor to review your financial plan and make adjustments as needed, especially during times of market volatility.

Conclusion

Social influences play a significant role in shaping financial behavior and decisions. Understanding the impact of social norms, peer pressure, herd behavior, and the influence of media and social networks is crucial for making informed and rational financial choices. By recognizing these influences and implementing strategies to manage them effectively, individuals can improve their financial behavior and achieve greater financial success. This chapter has explored the various social influences on financial behavior, providing insights and practical strategies for managing these influences. By applying these strategies, individuals can navigate their financial journey with greater confidence and resilience.

CHAPTER 12

HOW THE PSYCHOLOGY OF MONEY EXAMINES FEELINGS SUCH AS FEAR, GREED, JOY, AND STRESS INFLUENCE FINANCIAL DECISIONS AND BEHAVIOR

The psychology of money delves into how emotions such as fear, greed, joy, and stress influence financial decisions and behaviors. These emotions can drive individuals to make decisions that are not always rational or in their best interest. Understanding how these feelings impact financial behavior is essential for making more informed and effective financial choices. This chapter examines how fear, greed, joy, and stress affect financial decisions and behaviors and offers strategies for managing these emotions to improve financial outcomes.

The Influence of Fear on Financial Decisions

Fear is a powerful emotion that can significantly impact financial behavior. It often leads to risk-averse behavior and can cause individuals to avoid making necessary financial decisions.

Manifestations of Fear in Financial Behavior

1. Avoidance of Investment: Fear of losing money can lead to a reluctance to invest, resulting in missed opportunities for growth.

2. Hoarding Cash: Individuals may keep excessive amounts of cash instead of investing it, which can erode value over time due to inflation.

3. Financial Procrastination: Fear of making financial mistakes can lead to procrastination and avoidance of financial planning tasks.

Example: During an economic downturn, fear might cause an individual to withdraw from the stock market and keep their money in a low-interest savings account, missing out on potential recovery gains.

Strategies to Manage Fear

1. Education and Research: Increase your financial knowledge to reduce uncertainty and build confidence in your decisions.

- Example: Take a course on investment basics to understand different asset classes and their risk profiles.

2. Diversification: Spread investments across various asset classes to mitigate risk and reduce fear of loss.

- Example: Create a diversified portfolio that includes stocks, bonds, and real estate to balance risk and reward.

3. Consult with Advisors: Seek professional financial advice to make informed decisions and alleviate fears.

- Example: Work with a financial advisor to develop a long-term investment strategy that aligns with your risk tolerance.

The Influence of Greed on Financial Decisions

Greed, or the excessive desire for wealth, can drive individuals to take on significant risks in pursuit of high returns. It often leads to speculative investments and short-term thinking.

Manifestations of Greed in Financial Behavior

1. Speculative Investments: Greed can lead to investing in high-risk, high-reward opportunities without thorough research.

2. Overleveraging: The desire for quick profits can result in borrowing excessively to invest, increasing financial vulnerability.

3. Chasing Trends: Greed can cause individuals to follow investment fads, often buying high and selling low.

Example: An investor might pour all their money into a speculative stock or cryptocurrency, driven by the hope of substantial returns, without considering the potential for significant loss.

Strategies to Manage Greed

1. Set Clear Goals: Define long-term financial goals to focus on sustainable growth rather than short-term gains.

   - Example: Create a financial plan that prioritizes long-term wealth building, such as saving for retirement or buying a home.

2. Adopt a Long-Term Perspective: Focus on long-term investment strategies rather than short-term speculative gains.

   - Example: Invest in a diversified portfolio of stocks and bonds, aiming for steady growth over time.

3. Implement Risk Management: Use risk management techniques to limit exposure to high-risk investments.

   - Example: Set limits on the amount of money allocated to speculative investments and use stop-loss orders to manage potential losses.

The Influence of Joy and Excitement on Financial Decisions

Positive emotions like joy and excitement can lead to impulsive spending and overconfidence in investment decisions. While these feelings can drive positive action, they can also result in financial mistakes if not managed properly.

Manifestations of Joy and Excitement in Financial Behavior

1. Impulsive Spending: Joy and excitement can lead to unplanned purchases and overspending on non-essential items.

2. Overconfidence in Investments: Positive emotions can result in overconfidence, leading to risky investment decisions based on optimism rather than analysis.

3. Short-Term Gratification: The pursuit of immediate pleasure can overshadow long-term financial planning and savings.

Example: After receiving a bonus, an individual might go on a shopping spree or invest in a trendy stock without conducting proper research, driven by the excitement of having extra money.

Strategies to Manage Joy and Excitement

1. Budgeting and Planning: Create a budget that includes discretionary spending limits to manage impulsive purchases.

- Example: Allocate a specific amount of your bonus for fun spending, while saving or investing the remainder.

2. Practice Mindfulness: Develop mindfulness techniques to stay grounded and make more rational decisions.

- Example: Practice mindfulness meditation to maintain focus and avoid impulsive financial decisions driven by excitement.

3. Stick to a Plan: Follow a structured financial plan to stay focused on long-term goals despite short-term emotions.

- Example: Refer to your financial plan when making decisions about spending or investing, ensuring alignment with your long-term objectives.

The Influence of Stress on Financial Decisions

Stress related to money can lead to poor financial decision-making, such as avoiding financial responsibilities, making hasty choices, or engaging in unhealthy coping mechanisms.

Manifestations of Stress in Financial Behavior

1. Financial Avoidance: Stress can lead to avoidance of financial tasks, such as budgeting, investing, or addressing debt.

2. Hasty Decisions: Stress can cause individuals to make quick, emotion-driven decisions without fully considering the consequences.

3. Unhealthy Coping Mechanisms: Stress may lead to behaviors like retail therapy, where spending is used as a way to alleviate emotional distress.

Example: An individual stressed about mounting credit card debt might avoid looking at their statements, leading to missed payments and increased interest charges.

Strategies to Manage Stress

1. Financial Planning: Develop a comprehensive financial plan to provide structure and reduce uncertainty.

- Example: Work with a financial advisor to create a plan that addresses debt management, savings, and investment goals.

2. Stress-Reduction Techniques: Practice stress-reduction techniques, such as exercise, meditation, and deep breathing, to manage anxiety.

- Example: Incorporate regular exercise and mindfulness practices into your routine to alleviate financial stress.

3. Seek Support: Engage with financial advisors, support groups, or therapists to address financial stress and develop healthy coping mechanisms.

- Example: Join a financial literacy group to share experiences and gain support from others facing similar financial challenges.

Integrating Emotional Management into Financial Planning

Effectively managing emotions is crucial for making sound financial decisions. By integrating emotional management strategies into financial planning, individuals can improve their financial behavior and outcomes.

Developing Emotional Awareness

Recognize and understand your emotions and how they influence your financial decisions. This awareness is the first step toward managing emotional responses effectively.

Example: Keep a journal of your financial decisions and the emotions you felt at the time. Reflect on how these emotions influenced your choices.

Setting Clear Financial Goals

Having clear financial goals provides a framework for decision-making and helps you stay focused on long-term objectives rather than short-term emotional reactions.

Example: Write down your financial goals, such as saving for a home or retirement, and create a plan to achieve them. Refer to this plan during periods of market volatility.

Practicing Mindfulness and Stress Reduction

Mindfulness and stress-reduction techniques, such as meditation and deep breathing exercises, can help manage emotional reactions to financial situations.

Example: Practice mindfulness meditation for a few minutes each day to stay calm and focused, especially during periods of financial uncertainty.

Creating and Following a Budget

A well-defined budget helps manage spending and ensures that financial decisions align with your goals and values, reducing the impact of impulsive emotional spending.

Example: Use a budgeting app to track your income and expenses, setting limits on discretionary spending to avoid impulsive purchases.

Consulting with Financial Advisors

Financial advisors can provide an objective perspective and help you make decisions based on logic and analysis rather than emotions.

Example: Schedule regular meetings with a financial advisor to review your financial plan and make adjustments as needed, especially during times of emotional stress.

Conclusion

Emotions such as fear, greed, joy, and stress significantly influence financial decisions and behaviors. Understanding how these feelings impact financial behavior is essential for making more informed and effective financial choices. By recognizing the psychological mechanisms underlying emotional responses and implementing strategies to manage emotions effectively, individuals can improve their financial behavior and achieve greater financial well-being. This chapter has explored how the psychology of money examines the influence of emotions on financial decisions, providing insights and practical strategies for managing emotions in financial decision-making. By applying these strategies, individuals can navigate their financial journey with greater confidence and resilience.

CHAPTER 13

BEHAVIORAL ECONOMICS

Behavioral economics combines insights from psychology and economics to explain why people sometimes make irrational financial decisions. Traditional economic theories often assume that individuals are rational actors who make decisions to maximize their utility. However, real-world behavior frequently deviates from this ideal due to the influence of cognitive biases, heuristics, and emotions. This chapter introduces key concepts in behavioral economics and examines how these factors lead to anomalies in financial markets, such as bubbles and crashes.

Heuristics in Financial Decision-Making

Heuristics are mental shortcuts or rules of thumb that individuals use to simplify decision-making. While heuristics can be useful in reducing the complexity of decisions, they can also lead to systematic errors and biases. In the context of finance, heuristics can influence investment choices and risk assessment.

Availability Heuristic

The availability heuristic leads individuals to base their judgments on information that is readily available or easily recalled. This can result in an overestimation of the likelihood of events that are more memorable or recent.

Example: After witnessing a stock market crash, an investor may overestimate the probability of another crash occurring soon, leading to overly conservative investment decisions.

Representativeness Heuristic

The representativeness heuristic involves making judgments based on how closely something matches a particular prototype or stereotype. In finance, this can lead to overgeneralization and incorrect assumptions about investments.

Example: An investor might assume that a small technology startup will perform as well as other successful tech giants, despite differences in fundamentals and market conditions.

Cognitive Biases and Their Impact

Cognitive biases are systematic patterns of deviation from rationality in judgment. These biases affect how individuals process information and make decisions, often leading to suboptimal financial outcomes. Here are some key cognitive biases that impact financial decision-making:

Overconfidence Bias

Overconfidence bias leads individuals to overestimate their knowledge, abilities, and the accuracy of their predictions. Overconfident investors may take on excessive risk, believing they can consistently outperform the market.

Example: An investor might trade frequently based on their perceived ability to time the market, often resulting in lower overall returns due to transaction costs and poor timing.

Anchoring Bias

Anchoring bias occurs when individuals rely too heavily on the first piece of information they encounter, even if it is irrelevant. In financial decision-making, this can lead to skewed judgments and suboptimal choices.

Example: An investor might anchor to a stock's initial price and ignore subsequent information that suggests a change in its value.

Confirmation Bias

Confirmation bias is the tendency to seek out and favor information that confirms one's preexisting beliefs while ignoring or dismissing contradictory evidence. This bias can lead to reinforced poor investment decisions.

Example: An investor who believes in the potential of a particular industry might only pay attention to positive news about companies in that sector, ignoring negative reports.

The Influence of Emotions on Decision-Making

Emotions play a significant role in financial decision-making. Fear, greed, excitement, and regret can significantly influence how individuals perceive risk and make financial choices. These emotional reactions can lead to irrational behaviors that deviate from optimal decision-making.

Fear

Fear can lead to risk-averse behavior, causing individuals to avoid investments or sell assets during market downturns to prevent further losses.

Example: During a market crash, fear-driven panic selling can exacerbate the decline in asset prices, leading to significant financial losses.

Greed

Greed can drive risk-seeking behavior and speculative investment, leading individuals to take on excessive risk in pursuit of high returns.

Example: During a market bubble, greed can lead investors to buy overvalued assets, contributing to the unsustainable rise in prices.

Regret

Regret is the emotion experienced when individuals realize that their decisions have led to undesirable outcomes. In finance, regret can lead to an aversion to making future decisions for fear of repeating past mistakes.

Example: An investor who experiences regret after a significant loss may become overly conservative in their future investment choices, avoiding potentially profitable opportunities.

Market Anomalies: Bubbles and Crashes

Behavioral economics helps explain why financial markets sometimes behave irrationally, leading to phenomena such as bubbles and crashes. These market anomalies are often driven by the collective impact of heuristics, biases, and emotions.

Market Bubbles

Market bubbles occur when asset prices are driven to unsustainable levels by collective investor enthusiasm and speculative trading. Cognitive biases like overconfidence, anchoring, and herd behavior contribute to the formation of bubbles.

Example: The dot-com bubble of the late 1990s was characterized by excessive investment in internet companies, driven by overconfidence in their growth potential and herd behavior among investors.

Market Crashes

Market crashes happen when the inflated prices of assets suddenly collapse, often triggered by a loss of investor confidence. Fear and panic selling can exacerbate market declines, leading to sharp drops in asset prices.

Example: The stock market crash of 1987, known as Black Monday, was driven by panic selling and a loss of confidence among investors, resulting in a dramatic decline in stock prices.

Strategies for Mitigating Behavioral Biases

While it is impossible to eliminate cognitive biases and emotional influences entirely, awareness and strategic interventions can help mitigate their impact on financial decision-making. Here are some strategies to reduce the influence of behavioral biases:

Diversification

Diversifying investments can help reduce the impact of individual biases on overall portfolio performance. By spreading investments across different asset classes and sectors, investors can protect themselves from the effects of overconfidence and confirmation bias.

Systematic Decision-Making

Adopting a systematic approach to financial decision-making can help counteract the influence of cognitive biases. This involves setting clear investment criteria, following a disciplined process, and relying on data-driven analysis rather than emotional or instinctual reactions.

Seeking Diverse Perspectives

Consulting with financial advisors or engaging in discussions with peers can provide alternative viewpoints and help counter confirmation bias. Diverse perspectives can challenge existing beliefs and lead to more balanced and informed decisions.

Continuous Education

Continuous learning about behavioral economics and cognitive biases can increase awareness and improve decision-making. Staying informed about the latest research and seeking educational resources can help individuals recognize and manage their biases.

Conclusion

Behavioral economics provides valuable insights into the psychological factors that drive financial decision-making. By understanding heuristics, cognitive biases, and the influence of emotions, investors can make more informed and rational choices. Awareness of these factors, coupled with disciplined and systematic approaches to investing, can lead to improved financial outcomes and greater market stability. This chapter has introduced the foundational concepts of behavioral economics, providing a basis for further exploration of psychological principles in finance.

CHAPTER 14

COGNITIVE BIASES IN FINANCIAL DECISION-MAKING

Cognitive biases are systematic patterns of deviation from norm or rationality in judgment. These biases affect how we process information, make decisions, and interpret outcomes. In finance, cognitive biases can lead to suboptimal investment choices, market anomalies, and financial mismanagement. This chapter explores common cognitive biases, including overconfidence, anchoring, confirmation bias, and loss aversion, and their impact on financial decisions. Real-world examples illustrate how these biases manifest in everyday financial behavior and market movements.

Overconfidence Bias

Overconfidence bias occurs when individuals overestimate their knowledge, abilities, and the accuracy of their predictions. This bias can lead to excessive risk-taking and poor investment performance.

Impact on Financial Decisions

Overconfident investors may believe they have superior insight or information, leading them to trade more frequently and take on higher levels of risk. They often underestimate the volatility of the market and overestimate their ability to predict market movements.

Example: An investor who consistently outperformed the market in a bull run might believe their success is due to their skill rather than favorable market conditions. This overconfidence can lead them to continue taking high risks, resulting in significant losses when the market conditions change.

Manifestation in Market Movements

Overconfidence can contribute to market bubbles as investors pour money into overvalued assets, believing they will continue to rise. When reality sets in, and the overvaluation becomes apparent, the bubble bursts, leading to sharp declines.

Example: The dot-com bubble of the late 1990s saw many investors overconfidently investing in internet stocks, driving prices to unsustainable levels. When the bubble burst, it resulted in massive financial losses.

Anchoring Bias

Anchoring bias occurs when individuals rely too heavily on the first piece of information they encounter (the "anchor") when making decisions. This initial information can unduly influence subsequent judgments and decisions.

Impact on Financial Decisions

In finance, anchoring can cause investors to fixate on specific numbers, such as the initial price at which they bought a stock, and make decisions based on that anchor rather than current market conditions or new information.

Example: An investor buys a stock at $50 and sees it drop to $30. Anchored to the original purchase price, they might hold onto the stock, hoping it will return to $50, even when evidence suggests that the stock is unlikely to recover.

Manifestation in Market Movements

Anchoring can lead to resistance to price changes, as investors cling to past price levels. This behavior can result in delayed market reactions to new information, contributing to inefficiencies.

Example: During earnings season, a company reports lower-than-expected profits. Investors anchored to the previous high stock price may be slow to adjust their expectations, leading to a gradual rather than immediate decline in the stock price.

Confirmation Bias

Confirmation bias is the tendency to seek out and favor information that confirms one's existing beliefs while ignoring or dismissing contradictory evidence. This bias can reinforce preexisting views and lead to overconfidence.

Impact on Financial Decisions

Investors with confirmation bias may selectively gather and interpret information that supports their investment choices, leading to skewed perceptions and decisions that are not based on a comprehensive analysis.

Example: An investor who believes in the long-term potential of renewable energy might only focus on positive news about the sector, ignoring warnings or negative reports. This selective attention can lead to an imbalanced portfolio and increased risk.

Manifestation in Market Movements

Confirmation bias can contribute to the persistence of trends, as investors reinforce each other's beliefs, driving prices higher or lower based on shared, selective information.

Example: During a bull market, confirmation bias can lead to collective over-optimism, with investors only paying attention to positive news and dismissing signs of an impending correction. This can prolong the rally and increase the eventual market correction's severity.

Loss Aversion

Loss aversion refers to the tendency to experience losses more intensely than gains of the same magnitude. This bias can lead to risk-averse behavior, as individuals go to great lengths to avoid losses, sometimes at the expense of potential gains.

Impact on Financial Decisions

Loss-averse investors may hold onto losing investments for too long to avoid realizing a loss, or they might avoid taking on new investments altogether due to fear of potential losses.

Example: An investor holds a stock that has declined significantly in value. Despite evidence that the stock is unlikely to recover, the investor refuses to sell it, hoping to avoid the psychological pain of acknowledging a loss.

Manifestation in Market Movements

Loss aversion can lead to market inertia, where investors are slow to respond to new information or trends due to fear of losses. It can also result in exaggerated market declines, as fear of losses prompts widespread selling.

Example: During a market downturn, the fear of further losses can lead to panic selling, exacerbating the decline as more investors rush to liquidate their holdings to avoid additional losses.

Strategies to Mitigate Cognitive Biases

While it is impossible to eliminate cognitive biases entirely, awareness and strategic interventions can help mitigate their impact on financial decision-making. Here are some strategies to reduce the influence of cognitive biases:

Diversification

Diversifying investments can help reduce the impact of individual biases on overall portfolio performance. By spreading investments across different asset classes and sectors, investors can protect themselves from the effects of overconfidence and confirmation bias.

Example: An investor with a diversified portfolio of stocks, bonds, and real estate is less likely to be severely affected by a downturn in any single asset class.

Systematic Decision-Making

Adopting a systematic approach to financial decision-making can help counteract the influence of cognitive biases. This involves setting clear investment criteria, following a disciplined process, and relying on data-driven analysis rather than emotional or instinctual reactions.

Example: An investor might develop a set of rules for when to buy or sell assets based on specific financial ratios and market conditions, reducing the likelihood of making decisions based on emotions or biases.

Seeking Diverse Perspectives

Consulting with financial advisors or engaging in discussions with peers can provide alternative viewpoints and help counter confirmation bias. Diverse perspectives can challenge existing beliefs and lead to more balanced and informed decisions.

Example: Regularly discussing investment strategies with a financial advisor or investment group can provide new insights and help identify potential blind spots influenced by cognitive biases.

Continuous Education

Continuous learning about cognitive biases and their impact on financial behavior can increase awareness and improve decision-making. Staying informed about behavioral finance research and seeking educational resources can help individuals recognize and manage their biases.

Example: Attending seminars, reading books, and following the latest research in behavioral finance can help investors become more aware of their biases and adopt strategies to mitigate their impact.

Conclusion

Cognitive biases are inherent in human decision-making processes and have a profound impact on financial behavior. By understanding these biases and their effects, investors can develop strategies to mitigate their influence and make more rational and informed financial decisions. Awareness of cognitive biases, coupled with disciplined and systematic approaches to investing, can lead to improved financial outcomes and greater market stability. This chapter has explored common cognitive biases, including overconfidence, anchoring, confirmation bias, and loss aversion, providing real-world examples to illustrate how these biases manifest in everyday financial behavior and market movements.

CHAPTER 15

THE ROLE OF EMOTIONS IN FINANCE

Emotions play a significant role in financial decision-making. While traditional economic theories often assume that individuals are rational actors, real-world behavior frequently deviates from this ideal due to emotional influences. Understanding how emotions such as fear, greed, and excitement affect investment choices and market trends is crucial for making sound financial decisions. This chapter discusses the impact of various emotions on financial behavior and explores the concept of emotional intelligence and its importance in finance.

Fear

Fear is a powerful emotion that can lead to risk-averse behavior. In the context of finance, fear often manifests as a reluctance to invest or a tendency to sell assets during market downturns to avoid further losses. This can result in missed opportunities for gains and suboptimal investment performance.

Impact on Financial Decisions

Fear can cause investors to avoid taking necessary risks, leading to overly conservative investment strategies. During market downturns, fear-driven panic selling can exacerbate declines and lock in losses.

Example: During the 2008 financial crisis, many investors panicked and sold their stocks at a loss, fearing further declines. This widespread selling exacerbated the market downturn and led to significant financial losses for many individuals.

Manifestation in Market Trends

Fear can lead to sharp declines in asset prices during periods of market uncertainty. When fear spreads among investors, it can trigger widespread selling, contributing to market crashes.

Example: The COVID-19 pandemic in early 2020 led to a sudden and significant drop in global stock markets as fear of the unknown consequences drove investors to sell off assets rapidly.

Greed

Greed, or the desire for wealth and profit, can drive risk-seeking behavior and speculative investment. While a certain level of ambition is necessary for financial growth, excessive greed can lead to irrational decision-making and bubbles in asset prices.

Impact on Financial Decisions

Greed can cause investors to take on excessive risk in pursuit of high returns, often ignoring fundamental valuations and potential downsides.

Example: During the dot-com bubble of the late 1990s, many investors poured money into internet companies with little regard for their fundamental value, driven by the prospect of high returns. The subsequent market crash left many investors with substantial losses.

Manifestation in Market Trends

Greed can drive asset prices to unsustainable levels during market bubbles. As investors chase ever-higher returns, they bid up prices beyond what is justified by underlying fundamentals.

Example: The housing bubble of the mid-2000s was fueled by widespread optimism about rising home prices and the prospect of easy profits from real estate investments. The eventual burst of the bubble led to the 2008 financial crisis.

Excitement

Excitement and optimism can influence financial decisions by leading individuals to take on more risk than they might otherwise consider. Positive emotions can create a sense of overconfidence, causing investors to underestimate potential downsides.

Impact on Financial Decisions

Excitement can lead to increased trading activity and higher risk tolerance, as investors become more willing to take on speculative investments.

Example: During a bull market, widespread excitement and optimism can drive asset prices higher as investors become more willing to take on risk. This can lead to inflated valuations and eventual market corrections.

Manifestation in Market Trends

Excitement can contribute to market rallies as optimistic investors drive up asset prices. However, when the excitement fades, it can lead to sharp corrections as investors reassess their risk tolerance.

Example: The cryptocurrency boom of 2017 saw a surge in prices driven by excitement and optimism about the future of digital currencies. When the excitement waned, the market experienced a significant correction.

Regret

Regret is the emotion experienced when individuals realize that their decisions have led to undesirable outcomes. In finance, regret can lead to an aversion to making future decisions for fear of repeating past mistakes. This can result in overly cautious behavior and missed investment opportunities.

Impact on Financial Decisions

Regret can cause investors to avoid taking necessary risks or making new investments, leading to overly conservative strategies and potentially lower returns.

Example: An investor who experiences regret after a significant loss may become overly conservative in their future investment choices, avoiding potentially profitable opportunities due to fear of making another mistake.

Manifestation in Market Trends

Regret can lead to market inertia, where investors are slow to respond to new information or trends due to fear of repeating past mistakes. This can result in delayed market reactions and inefficiencies.

Example: After a market downturn, regretful investors may be hesitant to re-enter the market, leading to slower recovery and reduced market activity.

Emotional Intelligence in Finance

Emotional intelligence is the ability to recognize and manage one's emotions and the emotions of others. In finance, emotional intelligence is a valuable skill that can help individuals navigate the emotional ups and downs of investing and make more rational decisions.

Components of Emotional Intelligence

- Self-awareness: Recognizing one's emotional state and understanding how it influences decision-making.

- Self-regulation: Managing emotions to prevent them from leading to impulsive or irrational decisions.

- Motivation: Using emotions constructively to drive financial goals and objectives.

- Empathy: Understanding the emotions of others, which can be useful in negotiations and collaborative financial decisions.

- Social skills: Building strong relationships and networks that can provide support and diverse perspectives in financial decision-making.

Importance in Financial Decision-Making

High emotional intelligence allows investors to remain calm and focused during periods of market volatility, making more rational and measured decisions. It also enables individuals to manage stress and maintain a long-term perspective, avoiding impulsive reactions to short-term market movements.

Example: An investor with high emotional intelligence might stay calm during a market downturn, sticking to their investment strategy and avoiding panic selling. This disciplined approach can lead to better long-term outcomes.

Strategies for Managing Emotions in Finance

While it is impossible to eliminate emotions from financial decision-making, there are strategies that can help individuals manage their emotional responses and make more rational choices:

Establishing a Plan

Having a clear financial plan and investment strategy can provide a framework for decision-making, reducing the influence of emotions. A well-defined plan can help individuals stay focused on their long-term goals and avoid making impulsive decisions based on short-term market fluctuations.

Example: An investor with a diversified portfolio and a clear investment horizon is less likely to panic during market downturns, as they have a plan in place to weather short-term volatility.

Setting Limits

Setting predefined limits on investment decisions, such as stop-loss orders or maximum position sizes, can help mitigate the impact of emotions. These limits can act as safeguards, preventing individuals from making overly emotional decisions during periods of market stress.

Example: A stop-loss order automatically sells security when its price falls below a certain level, helping investors avoid large losses driven by emotional responses to market declines.

Practicing Mindfulness

Mindfulness techniques, such as meditation and deep breathing exercises, can help individuals manage stress and maintain emotional balance. Practicing mindfulness can improve emotional regulation and enhance decision-making under pressure.

Example: An investor who practices mindfulness may be better able to stay calm and focused during periods of market volatility, making more rational and measured decisions.

Seeking Professional Advice

Consulting with financial advisors or other professionals can provide an objective perspective and help counteract emotional biases. Advisors can offer guidance based on experience and expertise, helping individuals make informed decisions.

Example: A financial advisor can help an investor stay disciplined and focused on their long-term goals, even when emotions run high during market downturns or periods of exuberance.

Conclusion

Emotions play a crucial role in financial decision-making, influencing how individuals perceive risk, make investment choices, and react to market events. Understanding the impact of emotions such as fear, greed, excitement, and regret is essential for making more rational and informed financial decisions. By developing emotional intelligence and adopting strategies to manage emotional responses, individuals can improve their financial outcomes and navigate the complexities of the financial markets with greater confidence and stability. This chapter has explored the key emotional factors that affect financial behavior, providing a foundation for further exploration of psychological principles in finance.

CHAPTER 16

PSYCHOLOGICAL TRAPS IN INVESTING

Investors often fall into psychological traps that can undermine their financial success. These traps, which arise from cognitive biases and emotional influences, can lead to suboptimal investment decisions and financial losses. Understanding these psychological traps is crucial for making more informed and rational investment choices. This chapter identifies and analyzes common traps such as the disposition effect, mental accounting, and the endowment effect. It offers strategies to recognize and avoid these pitfalls to enhance investment outcomes.

The Disposition Effect

The disposition effect is the tendency of investors to sell assets that have increased in value while holding onto assets that have declined in value. This behavior is driven by the desire to realize gains and avoid realizing losses, often leading to suboptimal portfolio performance.

Impact on Financial Decisions

The disposition effect can cause investors to sell winning investments too soon, miss out on further gains, and hold onto losing investments too long, hoping they will rebound. This results in a portfolio skewed towards underperforming assets.

Example: An investor might sell a stock that has gained 20% to lock in the profit, but hold onto a stock that has lost 20% in the hope that it will recover, even when the fundamentals suggest otherwise.

Strategies to Avoid the Disposition Effect

- Set Clear Exit Criteria: Establish specific criteria for selling investments based on objective measures, such as reaching a target price or changes in fundamentals, rather than emotional responses.

- Rebalance Regularly: Periodically review and rebalance the portfolio to ensure it aligns with long-term goals and risk tolerance, regardless of short-term gains or losses.

- Use Stop-Loss Orders: Implement stop-loss orders to automatically sell investments that fall below a certain price, helping to avoid holding onto losing assets for too long.

Mental Accounting

Mental accounting refers to the tendency of individuals to categorize and treat money differently depending on its source, purpose, or intended use. This can lead to irrational financial behavior and misallocation of resources.

Impact on Financial Decisions

Mental accounting can cause investors to make inconsistent decisions, such as taking on higher risks with "found money" (e.g., bonuses or lottery winnings) while being overly conservative with savings.

Example: An investor might speculate with a tax refund by investing in high-risk stocks, viewing it as "extra money," while being very cautious with their regular savings.

Strategies to Avoid Mental Accounting

- Treat All Money Equally: View all financial resources as part of a single portfolio, regardless of their source, and make decisions based on overall financial goals and risk tolerance.

- Create a Comprehensive Financial Plan: Develop a holistic financial plan that integrates all sources of income and expenses, ensuring that decisions are made based on the entire financial picture.

- Seek Professional Advice: Consulting with a financial advisor can help provide an objective perspective and ensure that investment decisions are aligned with long-term goals rather than arbitrary mental categories.

The Endowment Effect

The endowment effect is the tendency to overvalue assets simply because they are owned. This bias can lead to irrational attachment to investments and reluctance to sell underperforming assets.

Impact on Financial Decisions

The endowment effect can cause investors to hold onto assets they own, even when it would be more rational to sell and invest the proceeds elsewhere. This behavior can result in missed opportunities and a suboptimal portfolio.

Example: An investor might hold onto a stock inherited from a family member, overvaluing it due to sentimental attachment, despite its poor performance and better alternatives available in the market.

Strategies to Avoid the Endowment Effect

- Regular Portfolio Review: Conduct regular reviews of the portfolio to objectively assess the performance of each investment and make decisions based on current fundamentals rather than emotional attachment.

- Consider Opportunity Cost: Evaluate investments in terms of their opportunity cost, comparing the potential returns of holding an asset versus selling it and investing in a more promising alternative.

- Set Investment Goals: Establish clear investment goals and criteria for evaluating assets, helping to ensure that decisions are driven by objective measures rather than emotional attachment.

Other Common Psychological Traps

Overtrading

Overtrading is the tendency to trade too frequently, driven by the desire to constantly take action or capitalize on short-term market movements. This behavior can lead to higher transaction costs and lower overall returns.

Example: An investor might frequently buy and sell stocks based on daily market news, incurring significant trading fees and potentially missing out on long-term gains from holding investments.

Strategies to Avoid Overtrading

- Adopt a Long-Term Perspective: Focus on long-term investment goals and resist the urge to react to short-term market fluctuations.

- Implement a Trading Plan: Develop a clear trading plan with specific criteria for buying and selling investments, reducing the impulse to trade based on emotions or market noise.

- Monitor Transaction Costs: Keep track of transaction costs and their impact on overall returns, helping to highlight the cost of overtrading and encourage more disciplined behavior.

Confirmation Bias

As discussed in previous chapters, confirmation bias is the tendency to seek out information that confirms existing beliefs while ignoring contradictory evidence. This can lead to reinforced poor investment decisions and overconfidence.

Example: An investor might only read positive news about a favored stock, ignoring warnings or negative reports that suggest it might be overvalued.

Strategies to Avoid Confirmation Bias

- Seek Diverse Perspectives: Actively seek out and consider alternative viewpoints and evidence that challenge existing beliefs, helping to ensure a more balanced and informed decision-making process.

- Conduct Comprehensive Research: Perform thorough research and analysis, considering both positive and negative information before making investment decisions.

- Consult with Advisors: Engage with financial advisors or investment groups to gain diverse perspectives and mitigate the influence of confirmation bias.

Conclusion

Psychological traps in investing, such as the disposition effect, mental accounting, the endowment effect, overtrading, and confirmation bias, can significantly impact financial decision-making and lead to suboptimal outcomes. By recognizing these traps and adopting strategies to mitigate their influence, investors can make more rational and informed decisions. This chapter has explored common psychological traps, providing insights and practical strategies to avoid these pitfalls and enhance investment success. Through disciplined and objective decision-making, investors can navigate the complexities of the financial markets with greater confidence and stability.

CHAPTER 17

SOCIAL INFLUENCES OR FINANCIAL BEHAVIOR

Human behavior is profoundly influenced by social factors, and financial decisions are no exception. Social norms, peer pressure, herd behavior, and the impact of media and social networks play significant roles in shaping how individuals and groups approach investing and financial management. Understanding these social influences is crucial for recognizing why people make certain financial choices and how these choices can affect broader market dynamics. This chapter examines these social influences and provides insights into their impact on financial behavior.

Social Norms

Social norms are the accepted behaviors and beliefs within a society or group. These norms can significantly influence financial decisions by establishing what is considered appropriate or desirable behavior.

Impact on Financial Decisions

Social norms can drive individuals to conform to the financial behaviors of their peers, even if those behaviors are not optimal. This can lead to decisions that are more about fitting in than about achieving the best financial outcomes.

Example: In a community where home ownership is highly valued, individuals might feel pressured to buy a house even if it is not the best financial decision for their situation, potentially leading to financial strain or debt.

Strategies to Recognize and Manage Social Norms

- Awareness and Education: Understanding the influence of social norms on financial decisions can help individuals make more informed choices based on personal financial goals rather than societal expectations.

- Objective Financial Planning: Developing a financial plan based on objective criteria and personal goals can provide a clear framework for decision-making, reducing the influence of social norms.

Peer Pressure

Peer pressure refers to the influence exerted by a peer group to encourage conformity to group behaviors and decisions. In finance, peer pressure can lead individuals to make investment choices based on what their friends, family, or colleagues are doing, rather than on their own research and analysis.

Impact on Financial Decisions

Peer pressure can result in individuals making investment decisions that they do not fully understand or that are not aligned with their risk tolerance and financial goals.

Example: An individual might invest in a particular stock or cryptocurrency because their friends are doing so, without conducting their own due diligence. This can lead to financial losses if the investment turns out to be risky or unsuitable.

Strategies to Mitigate Peer Pressure

- Independent Research: Conducting independent research and analysis can help individuals make informed decisions based on their own financial situation and goals.

- Setting Personal Financial Goals: Establishing clear financial goals and a strategy to achieve them can provide a framework for decision-making that is less influenced by peer pressure.

- Consulting Professionals: Seeking advice from financial advisors can provide an objective perspective and help counter the influence of peer pressure.

Herd Behavior

Herd behavior occurs when individuals mimic the actions of a larger group, often leading to market trends that are not based on fundamental values. This behavior can drive asset prices to unsustainable levels during market bubbles or lead to sharp declines during market crashes.

Impact on Financial Decisions

Herd behavior can lead to irrational investment decisions, as individuals follow the crowd without conducting their own analysis or considering the fundamentals.

Example: During the housing bubble of the mid-2000s, many people bought homes at inflated prices because everyone else was doing so. When the bubble burst, it led to significant financial losses and foreclosures.

Strategies to Avoid Herd Behavior

- Critical Thinking: Developing critical thinking skills can help individuals evaluate investments based on their own research and analysis rather than simply following the crowd.

- Diversification: Diversifying investments can help mitigate the impact of herd behavior by spreading risk across different asset classes and sectors.

- Long-Term Perspective: Focusing on long-term financial goals can help individuals avoid the temptation to follow short-term market trends driven by herd behavior.

The Impact of Media and Social Networks

Media and social networks play a significant role in shaping public perception and influencing financial decisions. News articles, social media posts, and financial influencers can all impact investor sentiment and drive market movements.

Media Influence

The media can amplify market trends by highlighting certain events, stocks, or economic indicators, leading to increased investor attention and action.

Example: Positive news coverage about a company can lead to a surge in its stock price as investors rush to buy shares. Conversely, negative news can lead to sharp declines as investors sell off assets.

Social Networks Influence

Social networks allow for rapid dissemination of information and can create echo chambers where certain viewpoints are reinforced. Financial decisions can be heavily influenced by the opinions and behaviors shared on these platforms.

Example: The GameStop short squeeze in early 2021 was largely driven by discussions and coordination among retail investors on social media platforms like Reddit. This collective action led to significant price volatility and market disruptions.

Strategies to Manage Media and Social Network Influence

- Verify Information: Always verify information from multiple reliable sources before making investment decisions based on media or social network inputs.

- Limit Exposure: Limiting exposure to financial news and social media can help reduce the emotional impact of sensational headlines and trending topics.

- Focus on Fundamentals: Base investment decisions on fundamental analysis and long-term financial goals rather than short-term media hype or social media trends.

Conclusion

Social influences play a significant role in shaping financial behavior and market dynamics. By understanding the impact of social norms, peer pressure, herd behavior, and the influence of media and social networks, individuals can develop strategies to make more informed and rational financial decisions. This chapter has examined these key social factors and provided practical strategies to recognize and manage their influence. By conducting independent research, setting personal financial goals, and focusing on long-term perspectives, investors can navigate the complexities of the financial markets with greater confidence and stability.

CHAPTER 18

THE PSYCHOLOGY OF RISK AND REWARD

Understanding how people perceive risk and reward is crucial for financial decision-making. Perceptions of risk and reward influence investment choices, risk tolerance, and financial behavior. This chapter delves into the psychological factors that shape risk tolerance and risk-taking behavior. It discusses concepts such as prospect theory, the role of uncertainty in financial choices, and how these elements interact to influence financial decisions.

Perception of Risk

Risk perception is the subjective judgment people make about the severity and probability of a risk. This perception is influenced by psychological factors, personal experiences, and cognitive biases.

Factors Influencing Risk Perception

- Personal Experience: Individuals who have experienced financial losses may perceive future risks as higher and be more risk-averse.

- Cognitive Biases: Biases such as overconfidence and anchoring can distort risk perception. Overconfident individuals may underestimate risks, while those influenced by anchoring might base their risk assessments on irrelevant initial information.

- Emotional State: Emotions such as fear and anxiety can heighten risk perception, leading to more conservative financial behavior.

Example: An investor who lost money in a previous market crash may perceive the stock market as riskier and prefer safer investments like bonds or savings accounts.

Risk Tolerance

Risk tolerance is the degree of variability in investment returns that an individual is willing to withstand. It is a crucial component of financial planning and investment strategy.

Psychological Factors Shaping Risk Tolerance

- Personality Traits: Traits such as optimism, pessimism, and sensation-seeking can influence risk tolerance.

Optimistic individuals may have higher risk tolerance, while pessimists may be more risk-averse.

- Financial Goals: Long-term goals and the timeframe for achieving them can affect risk tolerance. Individuals with long-term goals may be more willing to take on higher risks.

- Cognitive Processes: How individuals process information and evaluate potential outcomes can shape their risk tolerance. Analytical thinkers may have a more measured approach to risk, while intuitive thinkers may be influenced more by emotions.

Example: A young professional with a long investment horizon may have a higher risk tolerance and invest in stocks, while a retiree may prefer low-risk investments like bonds or annuities.

Prospect Theory

Prospect theory, developed by Daniel Kahneman and Amos Tversky, provides a framework for understanding how people make decisions involving risk and uncertainty. It challenges the traditional economic assumption that individuals are rational actors who always seek to maximize utility.

Key Concepts of Prospect Theory

- Value Function: The value function in prospect theory is defined over gains and losses rather than final wealth, and it is generally concave for gains and convex for losses. This reflects risk aversion for gains and risk-seeking behavior for losses.

- Loss Aversion: People tend to experience losses more intensely than gains of the same magnitude. This can lead to risk-averse behavior when facing potential gains and risk-seeking behavior when facing potential losses.

- Probability Weighting: Individuals tend to overweight small probabilities and underweight large probabilities, leading to decisions that deviate from expected utility theory.

Example: An investor may refuse to sell a declining stock to avoid realizing a loss (loss aversion), even if selling it would be the more rational choice based on future prospects.

The Role of Uncertainty

Uncertainty plays a significant role in financial decision-making. It refers to situations where the probabilities of outcomes are unknown, making it challenging to evaluate potential risks and rewards.

Managing Uncertainty

- Diversification: Diversifying investments across different asset classes and sectors can help manage uncertainty by spreading risk.

- Information Gathering: Seeking out and analyzing relevant information can reduce uncertainty and improve decision-making.

- Professional Advice: Consulting with financial advisors can provide expertise and insights that help navigate uncertain financial environments.

Example: During times of economic uncertainty, an investor might diversify their portfolio to include a mix of stocks, bonds, and real estate to mitigate risk.

Risk-Taking Behavior

Risk-taking behavior varies among individuals and is influenced by their risk perception, risk tolerance, and potential rewards. Understanding these behaviors is essential for developing effective investment strategies.

Factors Influencing Risk-Taking Behavior

- Potential Rewards: Higher potential rewards can incentivize greater risk-taking. Investors might be willing to take on more risk if the potential returns are substantial.

- Past Experiences: Previous successes or failures in risk-taking can shape future behavior. A successful high-risk investment might encourage more risk-taking, while a significant loss might lead to increased caution.

- Social Influences: Peer pressure and social norms can impact risk-taking behavior. Investors might take on more risk if they perceive it as a common practice among their peers.

Example: An entrepreneur might take on significant financial risk to start a new business, driven by the potential for high rewards and the encouragement of a supportive peer network.

Strategies for Balancing Risk and Reward

Balancing risk and reward is a fundamental aspect of financial decision-making. Effective strategies can help investors achieve their financial goals while managing potential risks.

Risk Assessment

Conducting a thorough risk assessment involves evaluating the potential risks and rewards of an investment. This includes analyzing market conditions, the financial health of companies, and economic indicators.

Example: Before investing in a new startup, an investor might assess the market potential, the startup's business model, and the experience of its management team to gauge the risks and potential rewards.

Setting Risk Limits

Establishing risk limits can help manage exposure to high-risk investments. This includes setting maximum investment amounts for high-risk assets and using stop-loss orders to limit potential losses.

Example: An investor might decide to allocate no more than 10% of their portfolio to high-risk stocks and set stop-loss orders at 10% below the purchase price to manage potential losses.

Long-Term Perspective

Adopting a long-term perspective can help mitigate the impact of short-term market volatility and focus on achieving long-term financial goals.

Example: An investor with a long-term perspective might continue to invest in a diversified portfolio of stocks and bonds, despite short-term market fluctuations, to achieve retirement savings goals.

Conclusion

The psychology of risk and reward is a crucial aspect of financial decision-making. Understanding how psychological factors shape risk perception, risk tolerance, and risk-taking behavior can help investors make more informed and rational choices. Concepts such as prospect theory and the role of uncertainty provide valuable insights into the complexities of financial decision-making. By adopting strategies for balancing risk and reward, such as conducting thorough risk assessments, setting risk limits, and maintaining a long-term perspective, investors can navigate the financial markets with greater confidence and achieve their financial goals. This chapter has explored the key psychological factors that influence risk and reward, providing a foundation for further exploration of financial psychology.

CHAPTER 19

THE FINANCIAL PERSONALITY

Each individual has a unique financial personality that influences their approach to money management and investment. Understanding these personality traits can help individuals make more informed and tailored financial decisions. This chapter explores different financial personality types and how they affect financial behavior. It provides tools for self-assessment and strategies for leveraging one's financial personality to achieve financial goals.

Understanding Financial Personality

A financial personality encompasses an individual's attitudes, behaviors, and preferences related to money management and investment. It is shaped by various factors, including upbringing, experiences, and inherent personality traits.

Key Components of Financial Personality

- Risk Tolerance: The degree of variability in investment returns that an individual is willing to withstand.

- Financial Goals: The specific objectives an individual aims to achieve through their financial decisions.

- Decision-Making Style: How individuals approach making financial decisions, whether analytically, emotionally, or impulsively.

- Saving and Spending Habits: Patterns of saving and spending money that reflect an individual's financial priorities and discipline.

Financial Personality Types

Different financial personality types exhibit distinct characteristics that influence their financial behavior. Understanding these types can help individuals identify their own tendencies and develop strategies to leverage their strengths and address their weaknesses.

The Saver

Savers are individuals who prioritize saving money and are often very disciplined in their financial habits. They tend to avoid debt and focus on building financial security.

Characteristics:

- High discipline in saving

- Aversion to debt

- Preference for low-risk investments

- Conservative spending habits

Impact on Financial Behavior:

- Savers may miss out on higher returns from riskier investments.

- They may prioritize financial security over potential growth opportunities.

Strategies for Savers:

- Consider diversifying investments to include a mix of low-risk and higher-risk assets.

- Set specific financial goals to balance saving with spending on experiences or investments that can enhance quality of life.

The Spender

Spenders enjoy spending money and may prioritize immediate gratification over long-term financial security. They may be more prone to accumulating debt and living beyond their means.

Characteristics:

- Enjoy spending money on goods and experiences

- Higher likelihood of accumulating debt

- Less focus on saving

- Impulsive spending habits

Impact on Financial Behavior:

- Spenders may struggle to build long-term financial security.

- They may face financial stress due to high levels of debt.

Strategies for Spenders:

- Create a budget to manage spending and prioritize saving.

- Set up automatic transfers to savings accounts to build financial discipline.

- Focus on building an emergency fund to provide a financial safety net.

The Investor

Investors are individuals who actively seek to grow their wealth through investments. They are willing to take on higher levels of risk in pursuit of higher returns.

Characteristics:

- Active interest in investment opportunities

- Willingness to take on risk for potential returns

- Focus on wealth-building

- Analytical approach to financial decisions

Impact on Financial Behavior:

- Investors may achieve higher returns but also face greater volatility and potential losses.

- They may spend significant time and effort managing their investments.

Strategies for Investors:

- Diversify investments to manage risk.

- Stay informed about market trends and opportunities.

- Set clear investment goals and timelines.

The Risk-Taker

Risk-takers are individuals who are comfortable with high levels of risk and may engage in speculative investments. They are driven by the potential for significant returns.

Characteristics:

- High tolerance for risk

- Willingness to engage in speculative investments

- Focus on high returns

- Adventurous financial behavior

Impact on Financial Behavior:

- Risk-takers may achieve substantial gains but also face significant losses.

- They may experience financial stress due to the volatility of their investments.

Strategies for Risk-Takers:

- Balance speculative investments with more stable, low-risk assets.

- Set risk limits to manage potential losses.

- Regularly review and adjust investment strategies based on performance and goals.

The Security Seeker

Security seekers prioritize financial stability and are highly risk-averse. They prefer low-risk investments and focus on preserving their wealth.

Characteristics:

- Strong focus on financial stability

- Preference for low-risk investments

- Conservative financial behavior

- Aversion to debt and risk

Impact on Financial Behavior:

- Security seekers may miss out on higher returns from riskier investments.

- They may prioritize financial security over potential growth opportunities.

Strategies for Security Seekers:

- Explore diversified investment options to achieve a balance between security and growth.

- Consider working with a financial advisor to develop a strategy that aligns with their risk tolerance and financial goals.

- Focus on building a well-rounded financial plan that includes saving, investing, and debt management.

Tools for Self-Assessment

Self-assessment tools can help individuals identify their financial personality type and understand how it influences their financial behavior. These tools can provide valuable insights and guide individuals in developing tailored financial strategies.

Financial Personality Quizzes

Financial personality quizzes are designed to assess an individual's attitudes, behaviors, and preferences related to money management and investment. These quizzes typically ask questions about spending habits, risk tolerance, and financial goals.

Example: A financial personality quiz might ask questions such as:

- How do you react to market volatility?

- What are your top financial priorities?

- How do you typically make financial decisions?

Risk Tolerance Assessments

Risk tolerance assessments evaluate an individual's comfort level with financial risk. These assessments can help determine the appropriate level of risk for investment portfolios and guide asset allocation decisions.

Example: A risk tolerance assessment might include questions about:

- Willingness to accept short-term losses for long-term gains

- Reaction to market downturns

- Investment goals and timelines

Leveraging Financial Personality to Achieve Financial Goals

Understanding one's financial personality can help individuals leverage their strengths and address their weaknesses to achieve financial goals. Tailored strategies can enhance financial decision-making and improve overall financial well-being.

Aligning Financial Strategies with Personality

- Savers: Create a balanced investment portfolio that includes both low-risk and higher-risk assets to achieve growth while maintaining financial security.

- Spenders: Implement budgeting and saving strategies to build financial discipline and reduce debt.

- Investors: Diversify investments and set clear goals to manage risk and optimize returns.

- Risk-Takers: Balance high-risk investments with stable assets and set risk limits to manage potential losses.

- Security Seekers: Develop a well-rounded financial plan that includes growth opportunities while maintaining a focus on stability.

Setting Clear Financial Goals

Setting clear financial goals can provide direction and motivation for making informed financial decisions. Goals should be specific, measurable, achievable, relevant, and time-bound (SMART).

Example:

- Short-Term Goals: Build an emergency fund, pay off credit card debt, save for a vacation.

- Long-Term Goals: Save for retirement, invest in a diversified portfolio, purchase a home.

Continuous Education and Improvement

Continuous education about personal finance, investment strategies, and financial planning can help individuals improve their financial decision-making and adapt to changing circumstances.

Example:

- Attend financial workshops and seminars.

- Read books and articles on personal finance and investing.

- Consult with financial advisors for personalized guidance.

Conclusion

Understanding and leveraging one's financial personality is crucial for making informed and effective financial decisions. By recognizing the characteristics and behaviors associated with different financial personality types, individuals can develop tailored strategies to achieve their financial goals. Self-assessment tools and continuous education can provide valuable insights and enhance financial decision-making. This chapter has explored the key components of financial personality, identified common personality types, and provided practical strategies for leveraging financial personality to achieve success. By aligning financial strategies with personal strengths and addressing potential weaknesses, individuals can navigate the complexities of financial management with greater confidence and success.

CHAPTER 20

THE IMPACT OF LIFE EVENTS ON FINANCIAL BEHAVIOR

Major life events, such as marriage, divorce, retirement, and economic crises, significantly impact financial behavior. These events often bring about substantial changes in financial circumstances, necessitating adjustments in financial planning and decision-making. Understanding the psychological effects of these events and how to manage finances through life's transitions is crucial for maintaining financial stability and achieving long-term financial goals. This chapter discusses the psychological effects of major life events and offers guidance on managing finances through these transitions.

Marriage

Marriage is a significant life event that often brings about changes in financial behavior. It involves combining finances, setting joint financial goals, and navigating new financial responsibilities.

Psychological Effects

- Increased Responsibility: Marriage often brings a sense of increased financial responsibility as individuals consider their partner's financial well-being in addition to their own.

- Financial Unity: Couples may experience a sense of unity and collaboration as they work together to achieve shared financial goals.

- Financial Stress: Disagreements about money can lead to financial stress and tension in the relationship.

Financial Management Strategies

- Open Communication: Establish open and honest communication about finances to ensure both partners are on the same page regarding financial goals and responsibilities.

- Joint Financial Planning: Develop a joint financial plan that outlines shared goals, budgets, and investment strategies.

- Separate and Joint Accounts: Consider maintaining separate accounts for individual expenses and a joint account for shared expenses to balance financial independence and unity.

Example: A couple might create a joint budget that includes individual spending allowances, shared household expenses, and contributions to joint savings goals such as a down payment on a house.

Divorce

Divorce is a challenging life event that can have significant financial implications. It often involves the division of assets, adjustments in income, and changes in financial responsibilities.

Psychological Effects

- Financial Anxiety: Divorce can lead to financial anxiety and uncertainty about the future, especially if one partner's income is significantly reduced.

- Loss of Financial Stability: The division of assets and changes in income can lead to a temporary loss of financial stability.

- Emotional Stress: The emotional stress of divorce can impact financial decision-making, leading to impulsive or irrational choices.

Financial Management Strategies

- Seek Professional Advice: Consult with financial advisors and legal professionals to navigate the division of assets and ensure a fair settlement.

- Create a Post-Divorce Budget: Develop a new budget that reflects changes in income and expenses, and prioritize rebuilding financial stability.

- Focus on Long-Term Goals: Set long-term financial goals to guide decision-making and provide a sense of direction during this transition.

Example: An individual going through a divorce might work with a financial advisor to develop a post-divorce financial plan that includes managing new living expenses, adjusting investment strategies, and planning for retirement.

Retirement

Retirement is a significant life event that marks the transition from active employment to a period of financial dependence on savings and investments. It requires careful financial planning to ensure long-term financial security.

Psychological Effects

- Shift in Financial Priorities: Retirement often involves a shift in financial priorities from wealth accumulation to wealth preservation and income generation.

- Adjustment to Fixed Income: Retirees must adjust to living on a fixed income from savings, investments, and pensions, which can be challenging.

- Sense of Security: Successfully transitioning to retirement can bring a sense of security and fulfillment.

Financial Management Strategies

- Retirement Planning: Develop a comprehensive retirement plan that includes income sources, expense projections, and strategies for managing healthcare costs.

- Diversify Income Sources: Ensure a diversified portfolio of income sources, including Social Security, pensions, and investment income, to provide financial stability.

- Adjust Spending: Adjust spending habits to align with the new fixed income, prioritizing essential expenses and finding ways to reduce discretionary spending.

Example: A retiree might work with a financial planner to create a detailed retirement budget that includes income from Social Security, pensions, and investments, along with strategies for managing healthcare expenses and preserving capital.

Economic Crises

Economic crises, such as recessions or market crashes, can have a profound impact on financial behavior. These events often lead to job losses, reduced income, and increased financial uncertainty.

Psychological Effects

- Financial Fear and Anxiety: Economic crises can trigger financial fear and anxiety, leading to conservative financial behavior and reduced spending.

- Risk Aversion: Individuals may become more risk-averse, avoiding investments and preferring to hold cash or low-risk assets.

- Adaptability: Successfully navigating economic crises can foster adaptability and resilience in financial behavior.

Financial Management Strategies

- Emergency Fund: Maintain an emergency fund to provide a financial safety net during periods of economic uncertainty.

- Review and Adjust: Regularly review and adjust financial plans and investment strategies to respond to changing economic conditions.

- Diversify Investments: Diversify investments across asset classes and sectors to manage risk and reduce the impact of market volatility.

Example: During an economic downturn, an individual might focus on building an emergency fund, reducing discretionary spending, and adjusting their investment portfolio to include more conservative assets.

Other Major Life Events

Job Loss

Job loss can lead to a sudden and significant change in financial circumstances, necessitating adjustments in budgeting and financial planning.

Strategies:

- Emergency Fund: Use the emergency fund to cover essential expenses while searching for new employment.

- Cut Expenses: Identify areas to cut expenses temporarily to conserve resources.

- Seek Support: Utilize unemployment benefits and seek support from career services to find new employment opportunities.

Birth of a Child

The birth of a child brings new financial responsibilities, including healthcare, education, and childcare expenses.

Strategies:

- Budget for New Expenses: Adjust the budget to include new child-related expenses.

- Save for Education: Start saving for the child's education early, using tax-advantaged accounts like 529 plans.

- Review Insurance: Ensure adequate health and life insurance coverage to protect the family's financial well-being.

Conclusion

Major life events such as marriage, divorce, retirement, and economic crises significantly impact financial behavior. These events often require adjustments in financial planning and decision-making to maintain financial stability and achieve long-term goals. By understanding the psychological effects of these events and adopting effective financial management strategies, individuals can navigate life's transitions with greater confidence and resilience. This chapter has provided insights into the impact of major life events on financial behavior and offered practical guidance for managing finances through these transitions. By preparing for and adapting to life's changes, individuals can achieve greater financial security and peace of mind.

CHAPTER 21

FINANCIAL EDUCATION AND PSYCHOLOGICAL WELL-BEING

Financial literacy is essential for making informed financial decisions and achieving psychological well-being. Understanding financial concepts and effectively managing money can significantly reduce financial stress, enhance financial stability, and improve overall mental health. This chapter highlights the importance of financial education and its role in reducing financial stress. It provides practical tips for improving financial literacy and fostering a healthy financial mindset.

The Importance of Financial Education

Financial education equips individuals with the knowledge and skills needed to make informed financial decisions. It covers a wide range of topics, including budgeting, saving, investing, debt management, and retirement planning. A solid foundation in financial literacy can lead to better financial outcomes and improved psychological well-being.

Benefits of Financial Education

- Informed Decision-Making: Financial education enables individuals to make informed decisions about their money, reducing the likelihood of financial mistakes and enhancing financial security.

- Reduced Financial Stress: Understanding financial concepts and having a clear financial plan can alleviate financial stress and anxiety.

- Improved Financial Health: Financially literate individuals are more likely to save, invest wisely, and manage debt effectively, leading to better financial health and stability.

- Empowerment and Confidence: Financial education empowers individuals to take control of their financial future, fostering confidence and a sense of autonomy.

Example: A person who understands the basics of budgeting, saving, and investing is more likely to make sound financial decisions, avoid debt, and build wealth over time.

Financial Stress and Psychological Well-being

Financial stress is a common issue that can significantly impact psychological well-being. It can arise from various factors, including debt, unexpected expenses, job loss, and inadequate savings. Financial stress can lead to anxiety, depression, and other mental health issues.

Sources of Financial Stress

- Debt: High levels of debt and difficulty in managing debt payments can cause significant financial stress.

- Unexpected Expenses: Unanticipated costs, such as medical bills or car repairs, can strain finances and lead to stress.

- Income Instability: Irregular income or job loss can create uncertainty and financial anxiety.

- Lack of Savings: Insufficient savings for emergencies or future goals can lead to financial insecurity and stress.

Example: An individual with substantial credit card debt and no emergency savings may experience chronic financial stress, leading to anxiety and difficulty concentrating.

Impact on Mental Health

- Anxiety and Depression: Financial stress is closely linked to anxiety and depression. The constant worry about money can lead to persistent feelings of helplessness and hopelessness.

- Sleep Problems: Financial concerns can cause sleep disturbances, leading to fatigue and reduced overall well-being.

- Relationship Strain: Financial stress can strain relationships, leading to conflicts and reduced emotional support.

Example: A couple experiencing financial difficulties may argue frequently about money, leading to relationship strain and additional stress.

Improving Financial Literacy

Improving financial literacy is a proactive step toward reducing financial stress and enhancing psychological well-being. It involves gaining knowledge about financial concepts and developing practical money management skills.

Practical Tips for Improving Financial Literacy

1. Educate Yourself: Take advantage of available resources such as books, online courses, workshops, and seminars to learn about personal finance topics.

- Example: Enroll in a personal finance course that covers budgeting, saving, investing, and debt management.

2. Create a Budget: Develop a detailed budget that outlines income, expenses, savings, and debt payments. Stick to the budget to ensure financial discipline.

- Example: Use budgeting apps or spreadsheets to track monthly income and expenses, adjusting as needed to stay within limits.

3. Build an Emergency Fund: Save a portion of your income in an emergency fund to cover unexpected expenses and reduce financial anxiety.

- Example: Aim to save at least three to six months' worth of living expenses in a separate savings account.

4. Manage Debt Wisely: Develop a plan to pay off high-interest debt and avoid accumulating new debt. Use strategies such as the snowball or avalanche method to tackle debt effectively.

- Example: Focus on paying off the credit card with the highest interest rate first while making minimum payments on other debts.

5. Invest for the Future: Learn about different investment options and develop a long-term investment strategy that aligns with your financial goals and risk tolerance.

- Example: Start investing in a diversified portfolio of stocks, bonds, and mutual funds to build wealth over time.

6. Seek Professional Advice: Consult with financial advisors or planners to get personalized advice and guidance on financial planning and investment strategies.

- Example: Schedule regular meetings with a financial advisor to review your financial plan and make adjustments as needed.

7. Stay Informed: Keep up with financial news and trends to stay informed about changes in the economy and financial markets.

- Example: Subscribe to reputable financial news sources and follow financial experts on social media.

Fostering a Healthy Financial Mindset

A healthy financial mindset involves adopting positive attitudes and behaviors toward money management. It requires self-awareness, discipline, and a proactive approach to financial planning.

Strategies for Fostering a Healthy Financial Mindset

1. Set Clear Financial Goals: Define short-term and long-term financial goals to provide direction and motivation for your financial decisions.

- Example: Set goals such as saving for a down payment on a house, paying off student loans, or building a retirement fund.

2. Practice Gratitude: Focus on appreciating what you have rather than constantly striving for more. This can reduce the urge for impulsive spending and promote financial contentment.

- Example: Keep a gratitude journal to regularly reflect on and appreciate the financial progress you have made.

3. Develop Financial Discipline: Cultivate habits of regular saving, budgeting, and mindful spending to maintain financial stability and achieve your goals.

 - Example: Automate savings contributions and bill payments to ensure consistent financial discipline.

4. Embrace Lifelong Learning: Continuously seek to improve your financial knowledge and skills to adapt to changing financial circumstances and opportunities.

 - Example: Attend financial workshops, read personal finance books, and participate in online financial communities.

5. Seek Support: Build a network of supportive friends, family, or financial mentors who can provide guidance and encouragement in your financial journey.

 - Example: Join a financial literacy group or community where you can share experiences and learn from others.

Conclusion

Financial education is essential for making informed financial decisions and achieving psychological well-being. By understanding financial concepts and developing practical money management skills, individuals can reduce financial stress, enhance financial stability, and improve overall mental health. This chapter has highlighted the importance of financial education and provided practical tips for improving financial literacy and fostering a healthy financial mindset. By adopting these strategies, individuals can take control of their financial future, achieve their financial goals, and experience greater peace of mind.

CHAPTER 22

STRATEGIES FOR OVERCOMING PSYCHOLOGICAL BARRIERS IN FIANCE

Overcoming psychological barriers is key to achieving financial success. Cognitive biases, emotional influences, and irrational behaviors can all hinder sound financial decision-making. This chapter offers practical strategies for mitigating the effects of cognitive biases, managing emotions, and making rational financial decisions. It emphasizes the importance of self-awareness, discipline, and continuous learning in finance.

Mitigating the Effects of Cognitive Biases

Cognitive biases are systematic patterns of deviation from rationality in judgment. They can lead to suboptimal financial decisions and hinder financial success.

Understanding and mitigating these biases is crucial for making informed and rational financial choices.

Common Cognitive Biases and Mitigation Strategies

1. Overconfidence Bias

Overconfidence bias leads individuals to overestimate their knowledge and abilities, resulting in excessive risk-taking and poor investment decisions.

Mitigation Strategies:

- Seek Diverse Perspectives: Consult with financial advisors and peers to gain different viewpoints and challenge your assumptions.

- Set Realistic Expectations: Base your investment goals on realistic assumptions and avoid overly optimistic projections.

- Keep Detailed Records: Maintain detailed records of your investment decisions and outcomes to objectively assess your performance.

Example: Before making a significant investment, consult with a financial advisor and review historical data to ensure your expectations are realistic.

2. Anchoring Bias

Anchoring bias occurs when individuals rely too heavily on the first piece of information they encounter, leading to skewed judgments.

Mitigation Strategies:

- Conduct Comprehensive Research: Gather and analyze information from multiple sources before making a decision.

- Question Initial Assumptions: Regularly question and reassess your initial assumptions in light of new information.

- Use a Structured Decision-Making Process: Follow a structured process that involves evaluating multiple factors and perspectives.

Example: When considering the purchase of a stock, research the company's financials, industry trends, and economic conditions rather than relying solely on its initial price.

3. Confirmation Bias

Confirmation bias is the tendency to seek out information that confirms existing beliefs while ignoring contradictory evidence.

Mitigation Strategies:

- Actively Seek Contradictory Information: Look for information that challenges your existing beliefs and consider alternative viewpoints.

- Engage in Critical Thinking: Evaluate the credibility and relevance of all information, regardless of whether it supports or contradicts your beliefs.

- Diversify Your Information Sources: Use a variety of reputable sources to gather information and avoid echo chambers.

Example: If you believe a particular sector is poised for growth, also research potential risks and negative trends in that sector to make a balanced decision.

4. Loss Aversion

Loss aversion is the tendency to experience losses more intensely than gains, leading to risk-averse behavior.

Mitigation Strategies:

- Focus on Long-Term Goals: Keep your long-term financial goals in mind to avoid making impulsive decisions based on short-term losses.

- Reframe Your Perspective: View potential losses as part of the investment process and focus on the overall growth of your portfolio.

- Set Predefined Risk Limits: Establish clear risk limits and stop-loss orders to manage potential losses without emotional interference.

Example: Regularly review your investment strategy to ensure it aligns with your long-term goals, even during market downturns.

Managing Emotions in Financial Decision-Making

Emotions play a significant role in financial decision-making. Fear, greed, excitement, and regret can all influence how individuals perceive risk and make financial choices. Managing these emotions is crucial for making rational financial decisions.

Strategies for Managing Emotions

1. Develop Emotional Awareness

Being aware of your emotions and how they influence your decisions is the first step in managing them effectively.

Example: Keep a journal of your financial decisions and note the emotions you experienced at the time. Reflect on how these emotions influenced your choices and outcomes.

2. Practice Mindfulness

Mindfulness techniques, such as meditation and deep breathing exercises, can help you stay calm and focused during periods of market volatility.

Example: Practice mindfulness meditation for a few minutes each day to improve your emotional regulation and decision-making under pressure.

3. Set Clear Financial Goals

Having clear financial goals provides a framework for decision-making and helps you stay focused on long-term objectives rather than short-term emotional reactions.

Example: Write down your financial goals and create a plan to achieve them. Refer to this plan during periods of market volatility to stay grounded.

4. Avoid Impulsive Decisions

Avoid making impulsive financial decisions based on emotions. Take time to assess the situation, gather information, and consider the potential consequences.

Example: If you feel the urge to sell an investment during a market downturn, take a step back and review your long-term investment strategy before taking action.

Making Rational Financial Decisions

Rational financial decision-making involves using logic and objective analysis to evaluate options and make choices that align with your financial goals.

Strategies for Rational Decision-Making

1. Conduct Thorough Research

Gather and analyze information from multiple sources to make informed decisions.

Example: Before investing in a new asset class, research its historical performance, risk factors, and potential returns.

2. Use a Decision-Making Framework

Follow a structured decision-making process that involves setting criteria, evaluating options, and considering potential outcomes.

Example: Create a checklist of factors to consider when making investment decisions, such as risk tolerance, time horizon, and financial goals.

3. Consult with Experts

Seek advice from financial professionals to gain objective insights and guidance.

Example: Schedule regular meetings with a financial advisor to review your investment strategy and make adjustments based on market conditions and personal circumstances.

4. Monitor and Review

Regularly monitor your financial decisions and review their outcomes to identify areas for improvement.

Example: Conduct quarterly reviews of your investment portfolio to assess its performance and make necessary adjustments.

The Importance of Self-Awareness, Discipline, and Continuous Learning

Self-awareness, discipline, and continuous learning are essential for overcoming psychological barriers and achieving financial success.

Self-Awareness

Self-awareness involves recognizing your strengths, weaknesses, and biases. It helps you understand how your personality and emotions influence your financial behavior.

Example: Take a financial personality quiz to identify your financial traits and tendencies. Use this information to develop strategies that leverage your strengths and address your weaknesses.

Discipline

Discipline involves sticking to your financial plan and making decisions based on logic and analysis rather than emotions.

Example: Set up automatic contributions to your savings and investment accounts to ensure consistent financial discipline.

Continuous Learning

Continuous learning involves staying informed about financial concepts, market trends, and investment strategies to make better decisions.

Example: Attend financial seminars, read books on personal finance, and follow reputable financial news sources to enhance your financial knowledge.

Conclusion

Overcoming psychological barriers is key to achieving financial success. By mitigating the effects of cognitive biases, managing emotions, and making rational financial decisions, individuals can improve their financial outcomes and achieve their long-term goals. This chapter has provided practical strategies for overcoming these barriers, emphasizing the importance of self-awareness, discipline, and continuous learning in finance. By adopting these strategies, individuals can navigate the complexities of the financial markets with greater confidence and resilience.

CHAPTER 24

THE RELATIONSHIP BETWEEN THE PSYCHOLOGY OF FINANCE AND THE PSYCHOLOGY OF MONEY

The fields of the psychology of finance and the psychology of money are closely related, yet they focus on different aspects of financial behavior and decision-making. Understanding the relationship between these two areas is essential for comprehensively grasping how individuals manage their finances and make financial decisions. This chapter explores the interconnectedness of the psychology of finance and the psychology of money, highlighting their differences, similarities, and combined impact on financial behavior.

Defining the Psychology of Finance

The psychology of finance examines how psychological factors influence financial decision-making, investment behaviors, and market dynamics. It focuses on understanding the cognitive biases, emotional influences, and social factors that affect how individuals and institutions make financial decisions.

Key Concepts in the Psychology of Finance

- Cognitive Biases: Systematic patterns of deviation from rationality in judgment, such as overconfidence, anchoring, and loss aversion.

- Emotional Influences: The impact of emotions like fear, greed, and excitement on financial decisions.

- Behavioral Economics: The integration of psychological insights into economic theory to explain why people sometimes make irrational financial decisions.

- Market Behavior: How collective behavior and social influences drive market trends, bubbles, and crashes.

Example: The psychology of finance explains why investors might overreact to short-term market fluctuations, leading to excessive buying during booms and panic selling during downturns.

Defining the Psychology of Money

The psychology of money delves into the individual and cultural meanings attached to money, how people think about and manage their personal finances, and the emotional and psychological impacts of money on their lives. It addresses broader aspects of money beyond investment decisions, including spending, saving, debt, and financial well-being.

Key Concepts in the Psychology of Money

- Money Attitudes: Individuals' beliefs and feelings about money, shaped by personal experiences and cultural influences.

- Financial Behavior: How people handle money, including spending, saving, budgeting, and borrowing.

- Financial Stress and Well-being: The psychological impact of financial status and money-related stress on overall well-being.

- Cultural and Social Influences: How societal norms and cultural background influence money attitudes and behaviors.

Example: The psychology of money explores why some people save diligently while others spend impulsively, and how financial stress can affect mental health and relationships.

Interconnectedness of the Psychology of Finance and the Psychology of Money

While the psychology of finance and the psychology of money focus on different aspects of financial behavior, they are deeply interconnected. Both fields contribute to a holistic understanding of how individuals interact with money and financial systems.

Overlapping Areas

1. Behavioral Influences: Both fields examine how cognitive biases and emotions influence financial decisions. For example, fear and greed can impact both investment choices (psychology of finance) and spending habits (psychology of money).

Example: Loss aversion, a concept from the psychology of finance, can explain why people avoid selling losing investments and why they might also be hesitant to spend money on discretionary purchases.

2. Financial Well-being: The psychology of money emphasizes financial well-being, which is also a concern in the psychology of finance. Sound financial decisions, as studied in the psychology of finance, contribute to overall financial well-being.

Example: Effective investment strategies (psychology of finance) can lead to financial security and reduced financial stress (psychology of money).

3. Cultural and Social Context: Both fields recognize the impact of cultural and social influences on financial behavior. Social norms and cultural background shape attitudes toward money and investment behaviors.

Example: In some cultures, collective financial behaviors, such as community savings groups, influence both personal financial management (psychology of money) and investment decisions (psychology of finance).

Complementary Insights

1. Holistic Financial Planning: Integrating insights from both fields leads to more comprehensive financial planning. Understanding cognitive biases and market behavior (psychology of finance) enhances investment strategies, while insights into money attitudes and financial well-being (psychology of money) ensure a balanced approach to spending, saving, and debt management.

Example: A holistic financial plan considers both effective investment diversification (psychology of finance) and maintaining a healthy balance between saving and spending to support overall well-being (psychology of money).

2. Personalized Financial Advice: Financial advisors can provide more tailored advice by incorporating knowledge from both fields. Recognizing individual money attitudes

(psychology of money) and cognitive biases (psychology of finance) allows for personalized financial strategies.

Example: An advisor might help a client overcome fear-based investment decisions (psychology of finance) while also addressing underlying anxiety about money (psychology of money).

Practical Applications

Improving Financial Decision-Making

- Self-Awareness: Encourage individuals to become aware of their cognitive biases and emotional influences on financial decisions. This awareness can lead to more rational and informed choices.

- Example: Educating investors about common biases, such as overconfidence and confirmation bias, can help them make more objective decisions.

- Emotional Regulation: Teach strategies for managing emotions, such as mindfulness and stress reduction techniques, to improve financial decision-making.

- Example: Mindfulness practices can help individuals remain calm during market volatility, leading to more disciplined investment behavior.

Enhancing Financial Well-being

- Financial Education: Provide education on both investment strategies (psychology of finance) and money management (psychology of money) to build comprehensive financial literacy.

- Example: Workshops that cover budgeting, saving, investing, and managing debt can equip individuals with the skills needed for financial success.

- Holistic Financial Planning: Encourage a balanced approach to financial planning that considers both short-term and long-term goals, integrating insights from both fields.

- Example: A financial plan that includes an emergency fund, retirement savings, and investment diversification addresses both immediate financial security and future growth.

Conclusion

The psychology of finance and the psychology of money are interconnected fields that together provide a comprehensive understanding of financial behavior. While the psychology of finance focuses on investment decisions and market behavior, the psychology of money addresses broader aspects of money management and financial well-being. Integrating insights from both fields enhances financial decision-making, promotes financial well-being, and leads to more effective financial planning. By understanding the relationship between these two areas, individuals can develop a holistic approach to managing their finances and achieving long-term financial success.

CHAPTER 25

FINANCIAL LITERACY AND ITS IMPORTANCE FOR SUCCESS

Financial literacy is the knowledge and understanding of financial concepts and the ability to use this knowledge to make informed and effective financial decisions. It encompasses a wide range of skills and knowledge areas, including budgeting, saving, investing, debt management, and retirement planning. Improving financial literacy is essential for achieving financial success and overall well-being. This chapter explores what financial literacy is, why it is necessary for success, and practical steps to improve it.

Defining Financial Literacy

Financial literacy refers to the ability to understand and apply various financial skills effectively. It includes the knowledge required to manage personal finances, make sound investment decisions, and plan for future financial needs.

Key Components of Financial Literacy

1. Budgeting: The ability to create and maintain a budget that tracks income, expenses, and savings goals.

2. Saving: Understanding the importance of saving for emergencies, short-term goals, and long-term objectives.

3. Investing: Knowledge of different investment options, risk management, and strategies for building wealth.

4. Debt Management: Skills to manage and reduce debt, including understanding interest rates, repayment strategies, and the impact of credit scores.

5. Retirement Planning: Planning for financial security in retirement, including understanding retirement accounts, pensions, and Social Security benefits.

6. Financial Decision-Making: The ability to make informed financial decisions based on an understanding of financial concepts and personal financial goals.

Example: A financially literate individual can create a budget that allocates funds for essential expenses, savings, and investments, while also managing debt and planning for retirement.

The Importance of Financial Literacy

Improving financial literacy is necessary for several reasons, each contributing to overall financial success and well-being.

Empowering Informed Decision-Making

Financial literacy empowers individuals to make informed decisions about their money. Understanding financial concepts enables individuals to evaluate options, assess risks, and make choices that align with their financial goals.

Example: A person with financial literacy can compare different mortgage options, understand the implications of interest rates, and choose the best mortgage for their financial situation.

Reducing Financial Stress

Financial stress is a common issue that can negatively impact mental and physical health. Financial literacy helps individuals manage their finances effectively, reducing financial stress and anxiety.

Example: By creating and following a budget, an individual can avoid overspending, manage debt, and build an emergency fund, which reduces financial stress.

Achieving Financial Goals

Financial literacy is crucial for setting and achieving financial goals. Whether it's buying a home, saving for education, or planning for retirement, financial literacy provides the knowledge and skills needed to reach these goals.

Example: A financially literate person can create a savings plan for a down payment on a house, invest for long-term growth, and ensure they have enough funds for retirement.

Preventing Financial Mistakes

Lack of financial literacy can lead to costly financial mistakes, such as falling into debt, making poor investment choices, or failing to save for emergencies. Financial literacy helps individuals avoid these pitfalls.

Example: Understanding the terms and conditions of a credit card can prevent an individual from accruing high-interest debt and damaging their credit score.

Enhancing Financial Independence

Financial literacy fosters financial independence by enabling individuals to manage their money effectively without relying on others. It promotes self-sufficiency and confidence in financial decision-making.

Example: A financially literate person can create a comprehensive financial plan that includes budgeting, saving, investing, and managing debt, leading to financial independence.

Practical Steps to Improve Financial Literacy

Improving financial literacy is an ongoing process that involves continuous learning and application of financial concepts. Here are practical steps to enhance financial literacy:

1. Educate Yourself

Take advantage of available resources to learn about personal finance topics. Books, online courses, workshops, and seminars can provide valuable knowledge.

Example: Enroll in a personal finance course that covers topics such as budgeting, saving, investing, and debt management.

2. Create a Budget

Develop a detailed budget that tracks income, expenses, and savings goals. Regularly review and adjust the budget to ensure it aligns with your financial goals.

Example: Use budgeting apps or spreadsheets to track monthly income and expenses, adjusting as needed to stay within limits.

3. Build an Emergency Fund

Save a portion of your income in an emergency fund to cover unexpected expenses and reduce financial anxiety.

Example: Aim to save at least three to six months' worth of living expenses in a separate savings account.

4. Manage Debt Wisely

Develop a plan to pay off high-interest debt and avoid accumulating new debt. Use strategies such as the snowball or avalanche method to tackle debt effectively.

Example: Focus on paying off the credit card with the highest interest rate first while making minimum payments on other debts.

5. Invest for the Future

Learn about different investment options and develop a long-term investment strategy that aligns with your financial goals and risk tolerance.

Example: Start investing in a diversified portfolio of stocks, bonds, and mutual funds to build wealth over time.

6. Seek Professional Advice

Consult with financial advisors or planners to get personalized advice and guidance on financial planning and investment strategies.

Example: Schedule regular meetings with a financial advisor to review your financial plan and make adjustments as needed.

7. Stay Informed

Keep up with financial news and trends to stay informed about changes in the economy and financial markets.

Example: Subscribe to reputable financial news sources and follow financial experts on social media.

Fostering a Healthy Financial Mindset

A healthy financial mindset involves adopting positive attitudes and behaviors toward money management. It requires self-awareness, discipline, and a proactive approach to financial planning.

Strategies for Fostering a Healthy Financial Mindset

1. Set Clear Financial Goals

Define short-term and long-term financial goals to provide direction and motivation for your financial decisions.

Example: Set goals such as saving for a down payment on a house, paying off student loans, or building a retirement fund.

2. Practice Gratitude

Focus on appreciating what you have rather than constantly striving for more. This can reduce the urge for impulsive spending and promote financial contentment.

Example: Keep a gratitude journal to regularly reflect on and appreciate the financial progress you have made.

3. Develop Financial Discipline

Cultivate habits of regular saving, budgeting, and mindful spending to maintain financial stability and achieve your goals.

Example: Automate savings contributions and bill payments to ensure consistent financial discipline.

4. Embrace Lifelong Learning

Continuously seek to improve your financial knowledge and skills to adapt to changing financial circumstances and opportunities.

Example: Attend financial workshops, read books on personal finance, and participate in online financial communities.

5. Seek Support

Build a network of supportive friends, family, or financial mentors who can provide guidance and encouragement in your financial journey.

Example: Join a financial literacy group or community where you can share experiences and learn from others.

Conclusion

Financial literacy is essential for making informed financial decisions and achieving financial success. By understanding financial concepts and developing practical money management skills, individuals can reduce financial stress, enhance financial stability, and improve overall well-being. This chapter has highlighted the importance of financial literacy and provided practical steps for improving it. By adopting these strategies, individuals can take control of their financial future, achieve their financial goals, and experience greater peace of mind.

204

CHAPTER 26

COGNITIVE BIASES IN MONEY MANAGEMENT

Cognitive biases are systematic patterns of deviation from rationality in judgment, which can significantly impact money management. These biases can lead to suboptimal financial decisions, such as overspending, inadequate saving, and poor investment choices. Understanding cognitive biases and learning how to mitigate their effects is essential for improving financial decision-making and achieving financial stability. This chapter explores common cognitive biases in money management, their impact on financial behavior, and strategies for recognizing and overcoming these biases.

Understanding Cognitive Biases

Cognitive biases are inherent tendencies that affect how we process information and make decisions. They arise from mental shortcuts, known as heuristics, that the brain uses to simplify complex information processing. While heuristics can be helpful, they can also lead to systematic errors in judgment.

Key Components of Cognitive Biases

1. Heuristics: Mental shortcuts that simplify decision-making but can lead to biases.

2. Emotional Influences: Emotions can exacerbate cognitive biases, leading to irrational financial decisions.

3. Social Influences: Social norms and peer pressure can reinforce cognitive biases, affecting financial behavior.

Example: Overconfidence bias, where individuals overestimate their financial knowledge and abilities, can lead to risky investments and poor financial decisions.

Common Cognitive Biases in Money Management

Several cognitive biases can influence financial decisions. Understanding these biases is the first step toward mitigating their impact.

1. Overconfidence Bias

Overconfidence bias leads individuals to overestimate their knowledge and abilities, resulting in excessive risk-taking and poor financial decisions.

Impact on Financial Behavior:

- Risky Investments: Overconfident individuals may engage in speculative investments without adequate research.

- Underestimating Risks: They may underestimate the likelihood of financial setbacks, leading to insufficient savings.

Example: An investor might believe they can consistently outperform the market and make risky trades without considering potential losses.

Mitigation Strategies:

- Seek Diverse Opinions: Consult with financial advisors and trusted individuals to gain different perspectives.

- Set Realistic Expectations: Base your investment goals on realistic assumptions and avoid overly optimistic projections.

- Keep Detailed Records: Maintain detailed records of your financial decisions and outcomes to objectively assess your performance.

2. Anchoring Bias

Anchoring bias occurs when individuals rely too heavily on the first piece of information they encounter, which can skew their financial decisions.

Impact on Financial Behavior:

- Skewed Spending: People might base their spending and saving decisions on initial prices or values, ignoring subsequent information.

- Outdated Strategies: They may hold onto outdated financial beliefs or strategies.

Example: A person might stick to an old budget or investment strategy, even when new financial information suggests a change is needed.

Mitigation Strategies:

- Update Information Regularly: Continuously seek out new financial information and adjust your decisions accordingly.

- Consider Multiple Data Points: Avoid making decisions based on a single piece of information by evaluating various factors.

- Reassess Regularly: Periodically review your financial strategies and be willing to make changes.

3. Confirmation Bias

Confirmation bias is the tendency to seek out information that confirms existing beliefs while ignoring or dismissing contradictory evidence.

Impact on Financial Behavior:

- Selective Information: Investors might only seek out positive news about their investments, ignoring warning signs.

- Reinforced Habits: Individuals may stick to ineffective financial habits because they only acknowledge supporting evidence.

Example: A person who believes in the long-term growth of a particular stock might ignore negative reports and continue investing, despite clear signs of decline.

Mitigation Strategies:

- Challenge Your Beliefs: Actively seek out information that contradicts your current financial beliefs and consider it objectively.

- Diversify Information Sources: Use multiple, credible sources to gather a balanced view.

- Engage in Critical Thinking: Evaluate all information critically, regardless of whether it supports or contradicts your beliefs.

4. Loss Aversion

Loss aversion refers to the tendency to experience losses more intensely than gains of the same magnitude, leading to risk-averse behavior.

Impact on Financial Behavior:

- Avoiding Losses: People may avoid selling losing investments to avoid realizing a loss.

- Missed Opportunities: They might pass up profitable opportunities due to fear of potential losses.

Example: An investor might hold onto a stock that has lost value, hoping it will rebound, rather than accepting the loss and reallocating the funds.

Mitigation Strategies:

- Focus on Long-Term Goals: Keep your long-term financial objectives in mind to avoid making decisions based on short-term losses.

- Reframe Your Perspective: View potential losses as part of the investment process and focus on overall portfolio performance.

- Set Predefined Rules: Establish clear rules for when to sell investments, such as stop-loss orders, to reduce emotional decision-making.

5. Mental Accounting

Mental accounting is the tendency to categorize money into different accounts based on subjective criteria, leading to irrational financial behavior.

Impact on Financial Behavior:

- Categorized Spending: People may treat money differently depending on its source or intended use, leading to suboptimal financial decisions.

- Uneven Resource Allocation: They might overspend "found money" like bonuses or gifts while being frugal with their regular income.

Example: An individual might splurge with a tax refund while being overly cautious with their paycheck.

Mitigation Strategies:

- Treat All Money Equally: View all financial resources as part of a single portfolio, regardless of their source.

- Create a Comprehensive Budget: Develop a budget that integrates all income and expenses to ensure consistent financial management.

- Prioritize Goals: Allocate money based on financial priorities rather than arbitrary categories.

6. The Endowment Effect

The endowment effect is the tendency to overvalue assets simply because they are owned, leading to irrational attachment and reluctance to sell.

Impact on Financial Behavior:

- Emotional Attachment: Investors may hold onto underperforming assets due to emotional attachment.

- Irrational Valuation: They might refuse to sell assets, even when it would be financially beneficial to do so.

Example: A person might keep a car they rarely use because of sentimental value, even though selling it would free up funds for better uses.

Mitigation Strategies:

- Objective Evaluation: Regularly assess the value and performance of your assets objectively.

- Consider Opportunity Cost: Evaluate the potential benefits of selling assets versus keeping them.

- Seek External Opinions: Consult with others to gain an unbiased perspective on your assets.

Recognizing and Overcoming Cognitive Biases

Recognizing cognitive biases is the first step toward overcoming them. By being aware of these biases, individuals can take proactive steps to mitigate their effects and make more rational financial decisions.

Strategies for Recognizing Cognitive Biases

1. Self-Reflection: Regularly reflect on your financial decisions and identify patterns that may indicate cognitive biases.

- Example: Keep a financial journal to track your decisions and the reasoning behind them. Review it periodically to identify any biases.

2. Seek Feedback: Engage with financial advisors, peers, or mentors to get feedback on your financial decisions.

- Example: Discuss your investment strategies with a financial advisor to identify any potential biases and get objective advice.

3. Continuous Education: Stay informed about cognitive biases and their impact on financial behavior through books, articles, and courses.

   - Example: Read books on behavioral finance to deepen your understanding of cognitive biases and how to overcome them.

Strategies for Overcoming Cognitive Biases

1. Develop a Structured Decision-Making Process: Follow a systematic approach to financial decision-making that includes gathering information, evaluating options, and considering potential outcomes.

   - Example: Use a decision matrix to weigh the pros and cons of different investment options before making a choice.

2. Set Clear Financial Goals: Establish specific, measurable, achievable, relevant, and time-bound (SMART) financial goals to guide your decisions.

   - Example: Set a goal to save a certain amount for retirement within a specified timeframe and create a plan to achieve it.

3. Diversify Your Portfolio: Diversify your investments to spread risk and reduce the impact of cognitive biases on your overall financial performance.

- Example: Invest in a mix of asset classes, such as stocks, bonds, and real estate, to minimize risk and maximize returns.

4. Use Technology: Leverage financial tools and technology to assist with decision-making and reduce the influence of cognitive biases.

- Example: Use budgeting apps to track expenses and investments automatically, helping you stay on top of your financial goals.

5. Practice Mindfulness: Develop mindfulness techniques to manage emotions and reduce impulsive decision-making.

- Example: Practice mindfulness meditation to stay calm and focused, especially during periods of market volatility.

Conclusion

Cognitive biases are inherent in human decision-making and can significantly impact money management. By understanding these biases and implementing strategies to mitigate their effects, individuals can make more rational and informed financial decisions. Recognizing cognitive biases, developing structured decision-making processes, and leveraging technology and professional advice are crucial steps toward overcoming these biases. This chapter has explored common cognitive biases in money management, their impact on financial behavior, and practical strategies for mitigating their effects. By applying these insights, individuals can enhance their financial well-being and achieve greater financial success.

CHAPTER 27

TIME DISCOUNTING

Time discounting is a concept in behavioral economics that describes how people tend to value immediate rewards more highly than future rewards. This preference for immediate gratification can significantly influence financial decisions and long-term planning. Understanding time discounting and its impact on financial behavior is crucial for making informed decisions that promote financial well-being. This chapter explores the concept of time discounting, its effects on financial decisions, and strategies to mitigate its influence for better long-term financial planning.

Understanding Time Discounting

Time discounting refers to the tendency to prefer smaller, immediate rewards over larger, delayed rewards. This phenomenon is rooted in human psychology and reflects a natural inclination to prioritize the present over the future.

Key Components of Time Discounting

1. Present Bias: The tendency to give stronger weight to payoffs that are closer to the present time compared to those in the future.

2. Discount Rate: The rate at which individuals devalue future rewards compared to immediate ones. A higher discount rate indicates a stronger preference for immediate rewards.

3. Hyperbolic Discounting: A specific form of time discounting where the discount rate decreases over time, meaning individuals are more likely to choose immediate rewards over short-term delays but are more patient over longer delays.

Example: Choosing to spend money on a luxury item now rather than saving it for future financial security exemplifies time discounting.

The Impact of Time Discounting on Financial Decisions

Time discounting can lead to a range of financial behaviors that prioritize short-term satisfaction at the expense of long-term benefits. Understanding these impacts is crucial for recognizing and mitigating time-discounting biases.

Short-Term Spending vs. Long-Term Saving

Individuals who exhibit strong present bias may struggle to save money for future needs, opting instead for immediate consumption.

Impact on Financial Behavior:

- Reduced Savings: Preference for immediate spending can lead to lower savings rates and inadequate preparation for future expenses.

- Impulse Purchases: Individuals may make impulsive purchases without considering their long-term financial goals.

Example: An individual might choose to spend their paycheck on dining out and entertainment rather than contributing to their retirement fund.

Investment Decisions

Time discounting can also affect investment decisions, leading individuals to prefer investments with quick returns over those with long-term growth potential.

Impact on Financial Behavior:

- High-Risk Investments: Preference for quick returns can lead to investments in high-risk assets that promise immediate gains.

- Short-Term Focus: Investors may prioritize short-term performance over long-term stability and growth.

Example: An investor might favor day trading or speculative stocks over a diversified portfolio designed for long-term growth.

Debt Management

Time discounting can influence borrowing behavior, leading individuals to take on debt for immediate gratification without fully considering the long-term repayment implications.

Impact on Financial Behavior:

- High-Interest Debt: Individuals may accumulate high-interest debt through credit cards or personal loans to finance immediate desires.

- Delayed Repayment: Preference for immediate consumption can lead to delayed debt repayment, resulting in higher interest costs over time.

Example: A person might use a credit card to finance a vacation, prioritizing the immediate enjoyment over the long-term financial burden of repaying the debt.

Strategies to Mitigate the Impact of Time Discounting

Recognizing the influence of time discounting on financial decisions is the first step toward mitigating its effects. Several strategies can help individuals make more balanced financial choices that align with their long-term goals.

1. Set Clear Long-Term Goals

Establishing clear, specific long-term financial goals can help counteract the preference for immediate rewards.

Steps to Take:

- Define Goals: Identify and articulate your long-term financial objectives, such as retirement savings, buying a home, or funding education.

- Create a Plan: Develop a detailed plan to achieve these goals, breaking them down into manageable steps.

Example: Set a goal to save a specific amount for retirement and create a monthly savings plan to reach that target.

2. Automate Savings and Investments

Automating savings and investments can help ensure consistent contributions to long-term financial goals, reducing the temptation to prioritize immediate spending.

Steps to Take:

- Automatic Transfers: Set up automatic transfers from your checking account to your savings or investment accounts.

- Employer-Sponsored Plans: Enroll in employer-sponsored retirement plans with automatic payroll deductions.

Example: Schedule automatic monthly transfers to a retirement account, ensuring consistent contributions regardless of short-term spending temptations.

3. Use Commitment Devices

Commitment devices are tools or strategies that help individuals commit to long-term goals by restricting their ability to choose immediate rewards.

Steps to Take:

- Time-Locked Accounts: Use savings accounts with withdrawal restrictions to reduce the temptation to access funds for immediate spending.

- Financial Contracts: Create binding agreements to save or invest a certain amount regularly.

Example: Open a certificate of deposit (CD) account with a penalty for early withdrawal, encouraging long-term savings.

4. Practice Mindfulness and Delayed Gratification

Developing mindfulness and the ability to delay gratification can help manage the emotional impulses that drive time discounting.

Steps to Take:

- Mindfulness Techniques: Practice mindfulness meditation and other techniques to enhance self-awareness and emotional regulation.

- Delayed Gratification Exercises: Engage in activities that train your ability to delay gratification, such as waiting a day before making a non-essential purchase.

Example: Before making an impulse purchase, practice mindfulness meditation to assess whether the purchase aligns with your long-term financial goals.

5. Regularly Review and Adjust Financial Plans

Regularly reviewing and adjusting your financial plans can help keep you focused on long-term goals and reduce the influence of time discounting.

Steps to Take:

- Monthly Check-Ins: Schedule monthly reviews of your financial plan to track progress and make necessary adjustments.

- Adjust Goals: Reassess and adjust your financial goals as needed to ensure they remain relevant and achievable.

Example: Review your investment portfolio quarterly to ensure it aligns with your long-term financial objectives and make adjustments based on market conditions and personal goals.

Conclusion

Time discounting is a common cognitive bias that influences financial decision-making by prioritizing immediate rewards over future benefits. Understanding its impact on spending, saving, investing, and debt management is crucial for making more balanced financial decisions. By setting clear long-term goals, automating savings and investments, using commitment devices, practicing mindfulness and delayed gratification, and regularly reviewing financial plans, individuals can mitigate the effects of time discounting and achieve greater financial stability and well-being. This chapter has explored the concept of time discounting, its effects on financial behavior, and practical strategies for managing its influence to promote long-term financial success.

CHAPTER 28

ANCHORING BIAS

Anchoring bias is a cognitive bias that occurs when individuals rely too heavily on an initial piece of information—the "anchor"—when making decisions. This bias can significantly influence financial behavior, leading to suboptimal decisions in spending, saving, investing, and budgeting. Understanding anchoring bias and learning how to mitigate its effects is crucial for making more rational and informed financial decisions. This chapter explores the concept of anchoring bias, its impact on money management, and strategies for recognizing and overcoming this bias.

Understanding Anchoring Bias

Anchoring bias occurs when individuals fixate on an initial piece of information, such as a price, value, or estimate, and use it as a reference point for subsequent judgments and decisions. This initial anchor can skew perceptions and lead to biased decision-making, even when additional information is available.

Key Components of Anchoring Bias

1. Initial Anchor: The first piece of information encountered, which sets a reference point for decision-making.

2. Adjustment: The tendency to make insufficient adjustments away from the anchor, leading to skewed judgments.

3. Persistence: The anchor's influence persists even when new information is provided.

Example: When buying a car, if the initial price quoted is $30,000, subsequent negotiations and evaluations may be unduly influenced by this anchor, even if the car's market value is lower.

The Impact of Anchoring Bias on Financial Decisions

Anchoring bias can affect various aspects of financial decision-making, from everyday spending to long-term investments. Recognizing its influence is essential for mitigating its impact and making more objective financial choices.

Spending and Purchasing Decisions

Anchoring bias often manifests in spending and purchasing decisions, where initial prices or discounts can influence perceptions of value and affordability.

Impact on Financial Behavior:

- Overpaying: Individuals may overpay for goods and services because the initial price sets a high reference point.

- Impulse Purchases: Discounts from an anchored price can create a perception of value, leading to impulse purchases.

Example: A shopper might see a jacket marked down from $200 to $150 and perceive it as a good deal, even if the jacket's actual value is closer to $100.

Saving and Budgeting

Anchoring bias can also affect saving and budgeting practices, particularly when initial estimates or past expenses serve as anchors for future financial planning.

Impact on Financial Behavior:

- Inadequate Adjustments: Individuals may fail to adequately adjust their savings goals or budgets based on changing financial circumstances.

- Skewed Budgeting: Initial budget categories and amounts can become fixed reference points, leading to rigid and potentially unrealistic budgeting.

Example: A person might set a monthly grocery budget based on past spending without considering changes in income or food prices, resulting in either overspending or unnecessary frugality.

Investing and Valuation

In the context of investing, anchoring bias can lead to distorted valuations and investment decisions based on initial stock prices, market predictions, or financial advice.

Impact on Financial Behavior:

- Stock Prices: Investors may fixate on the initial purchase price of a stock, affecting decisions to buy, sell, or hold.

- Market Predictions: Initial market forecasts can anchor expectations and influence investment strategies, even when new information suggests a different course of action.

Example: An investor might hold onto a stock that has declined in value because they anchor on the initial purchase price, hoping it will rebound to that level.

Strategies for Overcoming Anchoring Bias

Recognizing the influence of anchoring bias is the first step toward mitigating its effects. Several strategies can help individuals make more balanced and rational financial decisions by overcoming anchoring bias.

1. Conduct Independent Research

Conducting independent research can help counteract the influence of initial anchors by providing a broader perspective and additional information.

Steps to Take:

- Gather Multiple Data Points: Collect information from various sources to ensure a well-rounded understanding of the financial decision at hand.

- Verify Information: Cross-check initial anchors with current data and market conditions.

Example: Before making an investment, research the company's financial health, industry trends, and market conditions to avoid relying solely on the initial stock price.

2. Set Clear Financial Goals

Setting clear financial goals can provide a structured framework for decision-making, reducing the influence of arbitrary anchors.

Steps to Take:

- Define Objectives: Clearly define short-term and long-term financial goals based on personal values and priorities.

- Create a Plan: Develop a detailed plan to achieve these goals, using objective criteria rather than initial anchors.

Example: Set a savings goal for a down payment on a house based on realistic calculations of income, expenses, and housing market trends, rather than an initial price quote.

3. Regularly Reevaluate Financial Decisions

Regularly reevaluating financial decisions can help ensure they remain aligned with current information and long-term goals, reducing the impact of outdated anchors.

Steps to Take:

- Periodic Reviews: Schedule regular reviews of your financial plans, investments, and budgets to assess their relevance and accuracy.

- Adjust as Needed: Make adjustments based on new information, changes in financial circumstances, and evolving goals.

Example: Review your investment portfolio quarterly to ensure it aligns with your current financial goals and market conditions, making adjustments as needed.

4. Seek Diverse Perspectives

Consulting with financial advisors, peers, or mentors can provide diverse perspectives and reduce the reliance on initial anchors.

Steps to Take:

- Engage Experts: Seek advice from financial professionals to gain objective insights and guidance.

- Discuss with Peers: Share financial decisions with trusted friends or family members to gain different viewpoints.

Example: Before making a major financial decision, such as purchasing a home or investing in a new venture, discuss your plans with a financial advisor to get a balanced perspective.

5. Practice Mindfulness and Critical Thinking

Developing mindfulness and critical thinking skills can help manage the emotional and cognitive impulses that drive anchoring bias.

Steps to Take:

- Mindfulness Techniques: Practice mindfulness meditation and other techniques to enhance self-awareness and reduce impulsive decision-making.

- Critical Evaluation: Critically evaluate financial decisions by questioning initial anchors and considering alternative viewpoints.

Example: Before making a purchase based on an initial price, practice mindfulness meditation to assess whether the decision aligns with your long-term financial goals.

Integrating Strategies into Daily Financial Practices

Incorporating strategies to overcome anchoring bias into daily financial practices can enhance overall financial well-being and decision-making.

Daily Practices

1. Mindful Spending: Before making any purchase, pause and reflect on whether the price is influenced by an initial anchor or if it aligns with your financial goals.

   - Example: Before buying a discounted item, consider its actual value and whether it meets a genuine need or is influenced by the initial price.

2. Regular Research: Stay informed about financial markets, products, and services to ensure decisions are based on current information rather than outdated anchors.

   - Example: Read financial news and updates regularly to stay aware of market conditions and new investment opportunities.

Weekly Practices

1. Budget Review: Review your budget weekly to ensure spending and saving decisions are based on current financial circumstances and not fixed anchors.

   - Example: Adjust your grocery budget weekly based on actual spending and changing food prices.

2. Goal Setting: Reassess your short-term financial goals each week to ensure they remain relevant and achievable.

- Example: Set a weekly savings target based on your monthly income and expenses, and adjust as needed.

Monthly Practices

1. Financial Check-Ins: Conduct monthly financial check-ins to review your overall financial health, including savings, investments, and debt.

- Example: Review your investment portfolio monthly to ensure it aligns with your long-term financial objectives.

2. Diverse Consultations: Schedule monthly consultations with financial advisors or mentors to gain diverse perspectives and reduce the impact of anchoring bias.

- Example: Discuss your financial plans with a mentor each month to gain new insights and adjust your strategy as needed.

Conclusion

Anchoring bias is a common cognitive bias that can significantly influence financial decision-making by causing individuals to rely too heavily on initial information. Understanding its impact on spending, saving, investing, and budgeting is crucial for making more rational and informed financial decisions. By conducting independent research, setting clear financial goals, regularly reevaluating decisions, seeking diverse perspectives, and practicing mindfulness and critical thinking, individuals can mitigate the effects of anchoring bias and achieve greater financial stability and success. This chapter has explored the concept of anchoring bias, its effects on financial behavior, and practical strategies for overcoming this bias to promote better financial decision-making.

CHAPTER 29

STATUS QUO BIAS

Status quo bias is a cognitive bias that leads individuals to prefer maintaining their current situation rather than making changes, even when change may be beneficial. This bias can significantly impact financial decisions, leading to suboptimal outcomes in spending, saving, investing, and planning. Understanding status quo bias and learning how to mitigate its effects is crucial for improving financial decision-making and achieving long-term financial goals. This chapter explores the concept of status quo bias, its impact on money management, and strategies for recognizing and overcoming this bias.

Understanding Status Quo Bias

Status quo bias occurs when individuals prefer to keep things the same rather than making changes, often due to fear of the unknown, loss aversion, or cognitive inertia. This preference for the familiar can lead to inertia in decision-making, where individuals stick with their current financial practices even when better options are available.

Key Components of Status Quo Bias

1. Fear of Change: Reluctance to change due to uncertainty and the perceived risks associated with new choices.

2. Loss Aversion: The tendency to weigh potential losses more heavily than equivalent gains, leading to a preference for the current state.

3. Cognitive Inertia: The mental effort required to change can lead to a preference for maintaining the status quo.

Example: An individual might continue to keep their money in a low-interest savings account rather than exploring higher-yield investment options, despite the potential for greater returns.

The Impact of Status Quo Bias on Financial Decisions

Status quo bias can affect various aspects of financial decision-making, from everyday spending to long-term investments. Recognizing its influence is essential for mitigating its impact and making more proactive financial choices.

Spending and Purchasing Decisions

Status quo bias can lead individuals to stick with familiar spending habits and avoid exploring new ways to save money or optimize spending.

Impact on Financial Behavior:

- Routine Spending: People may continue spending money in the same ways, even if alternatives could provide better value.

- Missed Savings Opportunities: Individuals might ignore potential savings from switching providers or negotiating better deals.

Example: A person might continue to pay for a cable subscription they rarely use instead of switching to more cost-effective streaming services.

Saving and Budgeting

Status quo bias can also affect saving and budgeting practices, leading individuals to maintain their current financial habits without considering improvements.

Impact on Financial Behavior:

- Inadequate Savings: People may stick to their current saving patterns, even if they are insufficient for future needs.

- Outdated Budgets: Individuals might rely on old budgeting methods that no longer align with their financial goals or circumstances.

Example: A person might continue saving a fixed amount each month without reviewing whether this amount aligns with their changing financial goals or inflation rates.

Investing and Portfolio Management

In the context of investing, status quo bias can lead to inertia in portfolio management, where individuals stick with their existing investments rather than adjusting their portfolio to optimize returns.

Impact on Financial Behavior:

- Underperforming Investments: Investors may hold onto underperforming assets due to a preference for the familiar.

- Lack of Diversification: Individuals might avoid diversifying their portfolio, leading to increased risk and potential underperformance.

Example: An investor might continue holding a stock that has consistently underperformed rather than reallocating funds to more promising opportunities.

Strategies for Overcoming Status Quo Bias

Recognizing the influence of status quo bias is the first step toward mitigating its effects. Several strategies can help individuals make more proactive and rational financial decisions by overcoming status quo bias.

1. Conduct Regular Financial Reviews

Regularly reviewing your financial situation can help identify areas where maintaining the status quo may be detrimental and prompt necessary changes.

Steps to Take:

- Schedule Reviews: Set regular intervals (e.g., quarterly or annually) to review your financial plans, investments, and budgets.

- Assess Performance: Evaluate the performance of your current financial strategies and identify opportunities for improvement.

Example: Conduct an annual review of your investment portfolio to assess whether your current allocations align with your financial goals and market conditions.

2. Set Clear Financial Goals

Setting clear financial goals can provide motivation to make changes and move away from the status quo.

Steps to Take:

- Define Objectives: Clearly define your short-term and long-term financial goals based on personal values and priorities.

- Create a Plan: Develop a detailed plan to achieve these goals, identifying specific actions and timelines.

Example: Set a goal to increase your retirement savings by a certain percentage each year and create a plan to achieve this through regular contributions and investment adjustments.

3. Educate Yourself

Increasing your financial literacy can reduce the fear of change and provide the confidence needed to make informed decisions.

Steps to Take:

- Learn Continuously: Engage in continuous learning through financial courses, books, and reputable online resources.

- Seek Advice: Consult with financial advisors to gain expert insights and guidance on potential changes.

Example: Take a course on personal finance or investment strategies to understand the benefits of diversifying your portfolio and how to do it effectively.

4. Embrace Small Changes

Making small, incremental changes can reduce the fear and resistance associated with larger changes, making it easier to move away from the status quo.

Steps to Take:

- Start Small: Begin with small adjustments to your financial habits, gradually building up to more significant changes.

- Track Progress: Monitor the impact of these small changes to build confidence and demonstrate the benefits of moving away from the status quo.

Example: Start by reallocating a small portion of your savings into a higher-yield investment and gradually increase the amount as you become more comfortable with the new strategy.

5. Challenge the Status Quo

Actively questioning and challenging the status quo can help identify areas where change is beneficial and necessary.

Steps to Take:

- Reflect Regularly: Regularly reflect on your financial habits and ask yourself why you continue to follow them.

- Consider Alternatives: Explore and evaluate alternative financial strategies and practices that could improve your financial situation.

Example: Question why you continue to use a traditional savings account and explore alternative options like high-yield savings accounts or investment accounts.

Integrating Strategies into Daily Financial Practices

Incorporating strategies to overcome status quo bias into daily financial practices can enhance overall financial well-being and decision-making.

Daily Practices

1. Mindful Spending: Before making any purchase, consider whether it aligns with your financial goals or is simply a result of habitual spending.

- Example: Before buying lunch at your usual spot, consider preparing meals at home to save money and align with your financial goals.

2. Financial Awareness: Stay informed about financial products and services that could offer better value than your current choices.

- Example: Regularly read financial news and updates to stay aware of new savings and investment opportunities.

Weekly Practices

1. Budget Check-Ins: Review your budget weekly to ensure it reflects your current financial goals and circumstances.

- Example: Adjust your weekly grocery budget based on recent spending patterns and changes in food prices.

2. Small Financial Changes: Implement small financial changes each week to gradually move away from the status quo.

- Example: Each week, identify one small expense to cut back on and redirect those funds to your savings or investment account.

Monthly Practices

1. Financial Goals Review: Review your financial goals monthly to ensure they remain relevant and achievable.

- Example: Assess your progress toward your savings goals at the end of each month and adjust your plan as needed.

2. Consult with Advisors: Schedule monthly consultations with financial advisors or mentors to gain insights and guidance on potential changes.

- Example: Discuss your financial plans with a mentor each month to gain new perspectives and adjust your strategy as needed.

Conclusion

Status quo bias is a common cognitive bias that can significantly influence financial decision-making by causing individuals to prefer maintaining their current situation rather than making beneficial changes. Understanding its impact on spending, saving, investing, and planning is crucial for making more proactive and rational financial decisions. By conducting regular financial reviews, setting clear financial goals, educating yourself, embracing small changes, and challenging the status quo, individuals can mitigate the effects of status quo bias and achieve greater financial stability and success. This chapter has explored the concept of status quo bias, its effects on financial behavior, and practical strategies for overcoming this bias to promote better financial decision-making.

CHAPTER 30

SUNK COST FALLACY

The sunk cost fallacy is a cognitive bias that occurs when individuals continue investing in a decision based on the cumulative prior investment (time, money, effort) rather than the future benefits or costs. This fallacy can lead to irrational decision-making and suboptimal financial outcomes. Understanding the sunk cost fallacy and learning how to mitigate its effects is crucial for making more rational and informed financial decisions. This chapter explores the concept of the sunk cost fallacy, its impact on money management, and strategies for recognizing and overcoming this bias.

Understanding the Sunk Cost Fallacy

The sunk cost fallacy arises when individuals consider past investments in their decision-making process, even when those costs cannot be recovered. This leads to an irrational commitment to a course of action that may no longer be beneficial.

Key Components of the Sunk Cost Fallacy

1. Irrecoverable Costs: Costs that have already been incurred and cannot be recovered.

2. Emotional Attachment: The tendency to continue an endeavor due to emotional investment, even when it is not rational.

3. Misplaced Rationalization: Justifying continued investment based on past costs rather than prospects.

Example: Continuing to fund a failing business because of the significant time and money already invested, even when prospects for future success are bleak.

The Impact of the Sunk Cost Fallacy on Financial Decisions

The sunk cost fallacy can affect various aspects of financial decision-making, from everyday spending to long-term investments. Recognizing its influence is essential for mitigating its impact and making more rational financial choices.

Spending and Purchasing Decisions

The sunk cost fallacy often manifests in spending and purchasing decisions, where individuals continue to spend money on a product or service they have already invested in, despite diminishing returns.

Impact on Financial Behavior:

- Continued Spending: People may continue spending money on a product or service to justify the initial investment, even if it is no longer valuable.

- Increased Financial Losses: By not cutting losses, individuals may incur greater financial losses over time.

Example: Persisting with an expensive gym membership despite rarely using it, just because of the initial sign-up fee.

Saving and Budgeting

The sunk cost fallacy can also affect saving and budgeting practices, leading individuals to stick with financial plans or budgets that no longer serve their best interests.

Impact on Financial Behavior:

- Inflexible Budgets: Individuals may adhere to outdated budgets due to the time and effort invested in creating them, even when adjustments are needed.

- Missed Opportunities: Sticking to a rigid saving plan might prevent individuals from taking advantage of better financial opportunities.

Example: Continuing with an old savings plan that no longer aligns with current income levels or financial goals.

Investing and Portfolio Management

In the context of investing, the sunk cost fallacy can lead to poor investment decisions, where individuals hold onto underperforming assets due to the amount already invested.

Impact on Financial Behavior:

- Holding Losers: Investors may hold onto losing investments, hoping to recoup losses, instead of reallocating funds to better opportunities.

- Missed Gains: By not selling underperforming assets, investors miss out on potential gains from better-performing investments.

Example: Keeping a declining stock because of the initial purchase price and refusing to sell at a loss, even when the future outlook is poor.

Strategies for Overcoming the Sunk Cost Fallacy

Recognizing the influence of the sunk cost fallacy is the first step toward mitigating its effects. Several strategies can help individuals make more rational financial decisions by overcoming this bias.

1. Focus on Future Costs and Benefits

Shifting focus from past investments to future costs and benefits can help make more rational decisions.

Steps to Take:

- Future-Oriented Thinking: Evaluate decisions based on future potential rather than past investments.

- Cost-Benefit Analysis: Conduct a thorough cost-benefit analysis for current and future scenarios, disregarding sunk costs.

Example: When considering whether to continue funding a project, focus on the potential future returns rather than the money already spent.

2. Set Clear Decision-Making Criteria

Establishing clear criteria for decision-making can help avoid the influence of sunk costs.

Steps to Take:

- Define Exit Points: Set predefined criteria for when to abandon a project or investment.

- Objective Metrics: Use objective metrics, such as performance indicators, to guide decisions.

Example: Set a rule to sell a stock if it drops below a certain price, regardless of the initial investment.

3. Seek External Perspectives

Consulting with financial advisors, peers, or mentors can provide objective perspectives and reduce the influence of sunk costs.

Steps to Take:

- Financial Advisors: Seek advice from financial professionals to gain an unbiased view.

- Peer Discussions: Discuss decisions with trusted friends or family members to gain different viewpoints.

Example: Before deciding to continue investing in a declining asset, consult with a financial advisor to get an objective assessment.

4. Practice Mindfulness and Emotional Regulation

Developing mindfulness and emotional regulation can help manage the emotional attachment to sunk costs.

Steps to Take:

- Mindfulness Techniques: Practice mindfulness meditation to enhance self-awareness and emotional regulation.

- Emotional Reflection: Reflect on the emotions driving your decisions and recognize when they are influenced by sunk costs.

Example: Before making a financial decision, practice mindfulness to assess whether your choice is influenced by past investments or future potential.

5. Regularly Review and Adjust Financial Plans

Regularly reviewing and adjusting financial plans can help ensure they remain aligned with current goals and circumstances, reducing the impact of sunk costs.

Steps to Take:

- Periodic Reviews: Schedule regular reviews of your financial plans, investments, and budgets.

- Make Adjustments: Adjust your plans based on current information and future goals, not past investments.

Example: Conduct a quarterly review of your investment portfolio and reallocate funds based on current market conditions and future outlook.

Integrating Strategies into Daily Financial Practices

Incorporating strategies to overcome the sunk cost fallacy into daily financial practices can enhance overall financial well-being and decision-making.

Daily Practices

1. Mindful Spending: Before making any purchase, consider whether the decision is influenced by past investments or future benefits.

- Example: Before renewing a subscription, evaluate whether you still derive value from it or if you are influenced by the initial sign-up fee.

2. Future-Focused Thinking: Regularly remind yourself to focus on future costs and benefits rather than past investments.

   - Example: When faced with a financial decision, write down the future potential outcomes to keep your focus forward-looking.

Weekly Practices

1. Cost-Benefit Analysis: Conduct a weekly cost-benefit analysis for ongoing projects or investments to ensure they still align with your goals.

   - Example: Evaluate the benefits of continuing with a hobby or side project versus the costs involved.

2. Objective Reviews: Review your financial decisions weekly to ensure they are based on objective criteria rather than sunk costs.

   - Example: Assess your weekly spending to identify any decisions driven by past investments rather than current value.

Monthly Practices

1. Financial Health Check: Conduct a monthly financial health check to review your overall financial situation, including savings, investments, and debt.

- Example: Review your monthly bank statements, investment accounts, and debt balances to assess your financial health.

2. Consult with Advisors: Schedule monthly consultations with financial advisors or mentors to gain insights and guidance on potential changes.

- Example: Discuss your financial plans with a mentor each month to gain new perspectives and adjust your strategy as needed.

Conclusion

The sunk cost fallacy is a common cognitive bias that can significantly influence financial decision-making by causing individuals to consider past investments rather than future benefits. Understanding its impact on spending, saving, investing, and planning is crucial for making more rational and informed financial decisions. By focusing on future costs and benefits, setting clear decision-making criteria, seeking external perspectives, practicing mindfulness and emotional regulation, and regularly reviewing financial plans, individuals can mitigate the effects of the sunk cost fallacy and achieve greater financial stability and success. This chapter has explored the concept of the sunk cost fallacy, its effects on financial behavior, and practical strategies for overcoming this bias to promote better financial decision-making.

CONCLUSION

The Psychology of Finance by Dr. Maxwell Shimba

The interplay between psychology and finance reveals profound insights into how human behavior affects financial decisions and market dynamics. Throughout this book, we have explored the various psychological principles that drive our financial choices, including cognitive biases, emotional influences, social factors, and the concept of time discounting. By understanding these principles, we can make more informed financial decisions, improve our investment strategies, and better manage both personal and corporate finances.

Key Takeaways

Cognitive Biases

Cognitive biases are systematic patterns of deviation from norm or rationality in judgment. Recognizing common biases such as overconfidence, anchoring, confirmation bias, and loss aversion is essential for mitigating their impact on financial decisions. By implementing strategies to overcome these biases, such as seeking diverse opinions, setting clear financial goals, and practicing mindfulness, individuals can make more rational financial choices.

Emotional Influences

Emotions play a significant role in financial decision-making. Fear, greed, joy, and stress can all influence our investment choices and spending habits. Understanding these emotional drivers allows us to develop strategies to manage them effectively, such as practicing mindfulness, setting clear financial goals, and seeking professional advice. Emotional intelligence is crucial for making sound financial decisions and maintaining financial well-being.

Social Influences

Social factors, including social norms, peer pressure, and herd behavior, profoundly impact financial behavior. Media and social networks can amplify these influences, affecting market perceptions and investor behavior. By recognizing the impact of social influences and integrating strategies to manage them, such as seeking diverse perspectives and conducting independent research, individuals can make more balanced financial decisions.

Time Discounting and Sunk Cost Fallacy

Time discounting describes the tendency to prefer immediate rewards over future benefits, while the sunk cost fallacy involves continuing an investment based on past costs rather than future prospects. Both concepts highlight the importance of focusing on future potential rather than past investments or immediate gratification. Strategies to mitigate these biases include setting clear long-term goals, automating savings and investments, and conducting regular financial reviews.

Strategies for Effective Financial Management

1. Develop Emotional Awareness: Understanding how emotions influence financial decisions is crucial. Practicing mindfulness and emotional regulation can help manage emotional impulses and improve decision-making.

2. Conduct Regular Financial Reviews: Regularly reviewing and adjusting financial plans ensures they remain aligned with current goals and circumstances. This practice helps mitigate the impact of cognitive biases and promotes proactive financial management.

3. Seek Professional Advice: Consulting with financial advisors and mentors provides objective perspectives and

expert guidance. Professional advice can help individuals navigate complex financial decisions and develop effective strategies.

4. Set Clear Financial Goals: Establishing specific, measurable, achievable, relevant, and time-bound (SMART) financial goals provides a structured framework for decision-making. Clear goals help focus efforts and align financial behaviors with long-term objectives.

5. Embrace Continuous Learning: Staying informed about financial concepts, market trends, and behavioral finance principles is essential for making informed decisions. Continuous learning equips individuals with the knowledge needed to adapt to changing financial landscapes.

Final Thoughts

The psychology of finance is a fascinating field that uncovers the deep connections between human behavior and financial outcomes. By understanding the psychological principles that drive financial decisions, individuals can develop strategies to manage biases, emotions, and social influences effectively. This knowledge empowers individuals to make more rational, informed, and strategic financial choices, ultimately leading to greater financial stability and success.

As you apply the insights from this book, remember that financial well-being is a journey that requires continuous self-awareness, learning, and adaptation. By embracing the principles of the psychology of finance, you can navigate this journey with confidence and resilience, achieving your financial goals and enhancing your overall quality of life.

Dr. Maxwell Shimba

259